CW01496925

Cartomancy

Unlocking the Secrets of Divination Using Playing Cards

Your Free Gift
(only available for a limited time)

Thanks for getting this book! If you want to learn more about various spirituality topics, then join Mari Silva's community and get a free guided meditation MP3 for awakening your third eye. This guided meditation mp3 is designed to open and strengthen ones third eye so you can experience a higher state of consciousness. Simply visit the link below the image to get started.

https://spiritualityspot.com/meditation

Or, Scan the QR code!

Chapter One: The Art of Cartomancy

Tarot cards were used as a form of divination.

https://unsplash.com/photos/7s2jp7OVktg

Once Upon a Time in Europe...

The first time playing cards existed was in Europe in the 1360s, particularly in Eastern Germany and Central Italy. By 1371, these cards were in Spain, where they were known as *naïpes*, which the Spanish still call these cards to this day. Back then, Fernando de la Torre designed a special form of the cards. According to him, these cards made it possible to predict your fortunes. He told people they could figure out who yearned for them the most, who was the most admired and wanted, and many other things. The Spanish would refer to telling fortunes as *echar suertes*, which translates to "casting lots." This is the earliest record of this term being used relating to card playing.

It's not clear how people used cards to predict their fortunes. At least there were no clear explanations until over 150 years later. However, before then, the cards would be classed with dice and other divination methods as *sortilege*, a word for witchcraft, often explicitly used to describe divination. Giovanni Francesco Pico Della Mirandola, an Italian, wrote passionately against the craft of divination in 1506. In his writings, he included pictures that were part of card games, naming them abominable. 48 years later, Martin de Azpilcueta, a Spanish priest, would officially declare all cards (also known as cartas) as evil and the process of divination using these cards as sinful and subject to condemnation. Also, Juan Perez de Montalvàn believed that fortune-telling using cards was witchcraft.

Unfortunately, there was no clear description by any of these men about how the cards were used to predict fortunes. For this reason, it's unclear whether they were talking about cartomancy or condemning something else altogether. In the 16th century, certain books were dedicated to fortune telling, which you could use to understand the cards and other things like dice and spinners. These books had pictures on the cards, which didn't play a significant part in divination and couldn't be classified under cartomancy.

One popular, simple card fortune book printed in 1505 is the Mainzer Kartenlosbuch. This book connects every card of the 48 cards in the German deck with a fortune written in eight lines. Interestingly, these fortunes were simply adaptations from some other, earlier fortune book that was not based on cards. The way people would consult this book was to first draw a card and then look at the book to figure out their fortune. Alternatively, they would attach a spinner to the book, which was split into 48 different parts, each with the card's name. Many of these European books from the late 15th to the 16th century were produced and written in various languages.

Simultaneously, the first record of divination by tarot would be during that century. Teofilo Folengo, also known as Merlin Coccai, kept a record of this divination in his interesting allegory, Chaos del Triperuno, which he wrote in 1527. The participants in the reading had explained the meaning of the cards they had received to a character named Limerno. They wanted him to write sonnets for them based on the cards they had drawn. Limerno would go on to oblige them. This was a work of fiction, but then, it's clear that Teofilo had some ideas about how cards could be used to figure out what life may hold in store, and this is the ultimate goal of cartomancy. This is as good a time as any to specify that cartomancy should not be treated as a way to tell your fortune or predict to the letter how things will work out for you on a particular day or regarding a specific situation. Instead, think of the readings as more of a guide and not the ultimate law on what will befall you.

Another record on cartomancy is from 1538, thanks to Juan Luis Vives, who explained in writing that one could consider the picture on a card as a sign of their future. He wrote a scene showing two people playing cards which alluded to this idea. Granted, the concept of divination was casually touched upon in this scene, but that implies that this must have been a common thing that occurred back then. In those times, looking at the cards to learn things to come was not novel.

The First Recorded Readings

Actual card readings would begin to show up in the early 1600s. From these times, the earliest records of how to divine the future with cards exist, and among the earliest explanations of the process was written by Sir John Melton. He wrote Astrologaster, or, The Figure Caster, in 1620. He went on to talk about how Henry Cuffee met his end for being treasonous in 1601 and that some wizard had already predicted his death 20 years beforehand by using cards. The wizard had asked the unfortunate Henry to choose three cards from a deck with all Knaves. Then he placed the cards one after the other on the table, face down. After this, he was asked to pick one, then another, and look at the face of each card. The record states that when Henry looked at the cards, he wasn't seeing Knaves. His own face stared back at him from the first card, the second card showed his judge, and the final one had the scene where he would be executed in Tyburn.

In 1942, Sebastián Cirac Estopañán documented the Spanish Inquisition, and his work contains information on how 16th-century women practiced card reading. Still, these weren't in-depth descriptions, sadly. When Margarita de Borja was tried for witchcraft in Madrid from 1615 to 1617, she confessed that she helped her clients by reading cards for them. The way she described it, she'd recite an incantation to Saint Martha as she shuffled the cards first, then set the cards on the table in five rows of four cards each, all face-up. It was a good sign if the cards appeared in pairs (for instance, a Knave with a Knave or a Queen with a Queen). If they didn't, it was a bad omen.

Yet another person who was tried for witchcraft from 1631 to 1632 in Toledo was Mariá Castellanos. Her process also involved an incantation as she shuffled the cards and set twelve cards on the table. She aimed to see if the Jack and Knight of Clubs wound up beside each other. Tried in 1633, Lady Antonia Mejía de Acosta said she would remove the Nine of Clubs out of a 40-card deck and then shuffle the other 39 as she prayed. When she had finished, she would set out nine cards. If there were more Cups and Coins than Clubs and Swords, that was a good omen, but it was unfortunate if the cards didn't turn up that way.

There would be yet another witch trial that lasted from 1648 to 1649. The unfortunate victim of this trial was Lady María de Acevedo. Working with 41 cards, she could figure out what her significant other was up to whenever he went to the palace. She could tell what thoughts occupied his mind, and not only that, but she could also use the cards to influence him so that he would return to her after any argument they had. In fact, she shared a story of a woman who was married to a water bearer struggling to make ends meet. The woman needed to know if her husband had fallen for someone else. During the reading, the King of Cups and the Jack of Coins showing up together would be a good omen, as the former represented the husband while the latter was the wife. These cards together meant all was well on the love front. The woman shuffled the deck of cards and set them down one after the other in five rows, all face up. Sadly, she learned the worst from this reading. She would shuffle the cards three more times, yet the Knight of Cups and Jack of Coins never showed up as a pair. Go through the Spanish Inquisition, and you'll find many readings of this sort recorded up until the 19th century.

With time, the witches would work with the cards by shuffling them while praying or saying incantations, placing 13 cards on the table in a circle and one in the middle. The reading would be founded on the magical qualities of the first five cards drawn. Still, there's no further information about what would happen. In 1960, Dorman Newman of England created a deck of cards meant to be used for divination. His design had the fortunes written on the cards themselves. It would eventually be published once more, in 1711, by John Lenthall. These cards would wind up having several iterations.

Sometimes, what appeared to be a simple card game was actually divination. The popular game Solitaire, for instance, is thought of as initially having been a form of cartomancy. Solitaire is called *Reéssite* in France (a word that means "success"), and many people want to find out if they will attain success using the cards.

Solitaire wasn't the only version of divination, as there could be more than one "player" in a card reading. For instance, in Whartoniana, Miscellanies, in verse and prose, published in 1727, a chapter talks about a curious game known as Piquet. It was no ordinary game, as it involved divination on heart matters. The author wrote of his experience with a character named Theresius. He chose to visit this character because he was curious about his destiny. So, Theresius read his palm, cast lots based on astrology, and then asked the author to return the next day. The author obliged but was confused when Theresius asked him to play Piquet. He went along with it, and eventually, Theresius played the Queen of Hearts, which won him the game. When this happened, Theresius revealed to the author that if he intended to fall in love, it was important that he went after a woman who was more suited to him because, as he put it, "For if ever you attack the divine Pallas, you will infallibly lurch."

By 1730, cartomancy would be practiced with regular cards. The first depiction of this was in the English play Jack the Gyant-Killer. The author talked about using a deck of 52 cards. First, the reader would need to choose the Significator card after shuffling the deck, and then four Kings were assigned to this card. Then the deck needed to be cut. After this, the pack was laid out in at least three rows, and the Significator card had to be found. Once the card was spotted, the reader interpreted the surrounding cards. According to this play, the Spades were the only suit that meant bad luck.

About 20 years later, a document would describe another method of reading Tarot cards in Bologna. This method involved 35 cards split into groups of seven. The manuscript explains what each of the cards meant. Still, there's no straightforward narrative surrounding the groupings, so it's unclear if this was a commonly used method for cartomancy in Bologna in the 18th century. Eventually, the card readers in this region would opt to work with 45 cards out of 62 cards, but they'd never use the same cards across all spreads.

Later in the 1750s, cartomancy would be recorded again, this time by Oliver Goldsmith in his book The Vicar of Wakefield. He wrote that cartomancy was something to be considered admirable when a woman had the skill, one he deemed as valuable as reading, writing, music, and needlework, among other things. At this time, there was also a description of cartomancy in Russia written by Giacomo Casanova. He had a mistress named Zaïre — and she was only thirteen. He thought she was acting suspiciously and criticized her for constantly referencing the cards, which he claimed she would consult ten times daily. He claimed he would have stayed with her if it weren't for her "desperate jealousy" and "blind trust" of the cards. Apparently, this young girl had figured out how to tell what he'd been up to whenever he was out all night. He would eventually throw her cards into the fire.

The first record of cartomancy in France came in the 18th century in the form of a police record dated March 17, 1759. Two women were imprisoned for eight days because, according to the reports, they had scammed other people of their money by pretending to help them find whatever they'd lost using divination by cards. Then, in 1972 in Marseille, Anne Cauvin would also be sentenced. She endured being "exposed in shackles" for three days, with her head in a bonnet covered in tarot cards. They also put a sieve on her neck, and she had to remain this way for an hour each time before the executioner would step in to break the sieve and rip up the cards. Thus, at this time, it's evident that cartomancy was popular, but it was usually done in secret.

Out of the Darkness, into the Light

Jean-Baptiste Alliette, born 1738, died 1791, was known as Etteilla, his last name reversed. In a book Etteilla wrote the year he died, he talked about cartomancy, which he called "*cartonomancy.*" He claimed no one knew of the practice in France until three old people offered their services in 1751, 1752, and 1753. According to Etteilla, the clients of these strangers had to draw their cards one after the other, and all omens were interpreted according to suits. Drawing Hearts meant happiness, Diamonds meant country, Clubs meant money, and Spades implied sorrow.

Etteilla claimed that he was the one who elevated the practice of cartomancy by doing away with picking cards one after the other and, instead, conducting readings based on the entire deck laid out on the table. Obviously, from what you now know of the history of cartomancy, you can tell Etteilla was appropriating credit that wasn't his. However, you can agree that he was the first to put out a printed cartomancy methodology in 1770, which wasn't attached to a pack like the Newman-Lenthall deck of cards. His publication would prove very popular, and he was the one who gave each pip an interpretation rather than just working with a card or two based on the suit's meaning.

In Eteilla's first publication, he shared a method of working with 32 cards using a French Piquet deck with every pip except the ones from 2 to 6. He would also add another card as the generic Significator, which he eponymously named "the Etteilla." He gave each card its meaning and keyword. He shared valuable information about various layouts like squares (Zaïre's favorite) or fans. He also briefly touched on working with Tarot cards for divination. Still, he never gave an in-depth description of the process.

In 1772, Antoine Court de Gébelin worked with another author who remained anonymous to put out some essays on the Tarot and its esoteric significance. The anonymous author was responsible for crafting a method of cartomancy that would work with Tarot, prompting Etteilla to pivot to the Tarot itself and tout its benefits. He would make it more complicated by adding some astrology in conjunction with his custom design of the Tarot. After this, he would publish works criticizing others' approaches to the Tarot, and with his notoriety, he drew a bunch of devotees committed to learning from him between 1783 and 1791. Thanks to Eteilla's obvious narcissism and De Gébelin's essays, Europe would eventually become aware of Tarot and other related esoteric matters and cartomancy. Etteilla's devotees made it their mission to spread his ideas far and wide and, with them, his custom Tarot deck.

Marie-Ann Adélaïde Lenormand became the most famous cartomancer during France's Revolution. Born in 1772, she was known as Mademoiselle Lenormand, and she kept that title Mademoiselle until she died in 1843, as she never got married. Lenormand developed her reputation, much like Etteilla did, through self-promotion. When she was a teenager, she realized she was clairvoyant. Lenormand used that gift to make herself a fortune during the Revolution. She became even more famous when Empress Josephine reached out to her for her services, and from there, other members of high society reached out to her. Her clientele included those in the most influential and powerful social circles of the time. She would write that she had done work for some of the crème de la crème. However, today, it is known that she was a card reader for Josephine and Napoleon and the author of the popular Le Petit Lenormand and Le Grand Lenormand oracle cards. Even now, these cards are used in France and French-speaking places. Still, the odds are she didn't really have anything to do with the cards, and the manufacturers are simply making money from her name since she's long gone.

Cartomancy in Modern Times

In the 19th century, cartomancy with Tarot would become more popular, far more so than working with regular playing cards, Etteilla's cards, and Lenormand cards. The English considered Tarot as an occult matter. Arthur Edward Waite, an English mystic, had difficulty finding real Tarot cards, so he devised his pack for telling fortunes, working with Pamela Colman Smith, who handled the artwork. Smith came up with some beautiful designs, and thanks to this and the fact that all the pips had illustrations, Tarot would become the popular choice for cartomancy, especially in the anglophone world.

Over in France, the people use either 22 cards out of the Tarot de Marseille or standard playing cards. Come 1900, there was a more modern pack of Tarot, which had double-ended genre illustrations. Also, the pips were your usual Hearts, Spades, Diamonds, and Clubs. Oswald Wirth, an occultist, redesigned and printed the Tarot de Marseille Trumps in 1889. In 1927, he published a revised form that included text and which many cartomancers would adopt. Paul Marteau would direct Grimaud, a card-making firm, to revive the Tarot de Marseille in 1930. After this, Marteau published a guide to the new pack in 1949 entitled Le Tarot de Marseille. Cartomancy is practiced in many different styles, and it's still evolving. Every form of cartomancy springs from the English or French occult interests of the late 19th century — except for Bolognese Tarotmancy, of course.

Differences between Tarot Reading and Cartomancy

Tarot reading and cartomancy are about reading cards to figure out what the future could bring, but there's so much more involved. Tarot is well recognized, and the decks tend to be large with interesting cards rather than the sort you'd find in the common card decks. Plus, tarot card decks have Wands, Pentacles, Cups, and Swords *as suits.* You'll also find Knights and common Jacks, which aren't in your run-of-the-mill deck.

Cartomancy is card reading with regular cards. The Queens represent female energies, while the Kings represent masculine energies. The Jacks are youths and don't have a specific gender. Cartomancy can offer some accuracy when predicting when something will likely play out. Where the Tarot deck has 78 cards, cartomancy readings usually work with a standard deck of 52 cards. Also, you can expect the meanings you get from cartomancy to be more to the point than Tarot. If you want to understand the possible results of your situation, use Tarot. But to get specific answers, cartomancy is best.

One More Thing...

This is an excellent time to remind you that whether it's cartomancy or Tarot reading, you must understand that this practice isn't about accuracy in seeing the future or making predictions, so please do not base important life decisions on the cards alone. Instead, work with them as powerful guidance, growth, and self-discovery tools. When you do a reading or sit in one, you must understand all you're getting is a possible outcome or path heavily influenced by your present emotions and choices. This means the readings aren't set in stone — and that's likely a relief since it means you can always do something about negative readings.

Now that you know the rich origins of cards as divinatory tools, how do you choose the right deck before you start? How many decks are there? Which one's relevant? You're going to learn all this and more in the following chapter.

Chapter Two: Choosing a Deck

Traditional Decks Versus Modified and Specialized Decks

If you've ever played Poker or some other card game, you may not have realized then that you were playing with the original version of the tarot. This deck has 52 cards of four suits: Spades, Hearts, Diamonds, and Clubs. Each suit has numbered cards from 2 through 9, the Ace card, and the face cards, the King, Queen, and Jack. It is said that these suits are connected to the classical elements:

- Earth (Clubs)
- Air (Diamonds)
- Fire (Hearts)
- Water (Spades)

There are various designs of traditional playing card decks these days. One of the common traditional decks is the French-suited one. Clubs or clovers are known as *Trèfles,* Diamonds (or Tiles) are called *Carreaux,* Hearts are known as *Cœurs,* and Spades (or Pikes) are called *Piques.* The Queen or Lady card is the Dame, the King is the Roi, and the Jack or Knave is the Valet. There's also another card known as the Cavalier between the Queen and the Jack. The French-suited cards are common because their simple patterns make it easier to mass-produce them. It's also worth noting that the French connect their face cards to specific personalities. If you're interested, look at the correlations below:

Suits: Clubs, Diamonds, Hearts, Spades

Kings: Alexandre, César, Charles, David

Queens: Argine, Rachel, Judith, Pallas

Jacks: Lancelot, Hector, La Hire, Hogier

Then there are the Belgian-Genoese cards, the second most common traditional deck of cards worldwide. These cards don't have the names the French assign to the face cards. These cards became common in the Ottoman Empire when the rulership permitted card playing. Eventually, the cards would be found in the Middle East, North Africa, and the Balkans.

Modified decks are almost like traditional decks, but they're changed in some way to make them easier to use for cartomancy. For instance, some decks may have extra cards, or the artwork may be modified to flesh out the readings for more details. The specialized cards, however, are specifically for cartomancy, with beautiful, exquisite art that offers more meaning thanks to the symbolism of each element of the drawing on the card. You can also expect these decks to have extra cards and different suits.

Standard Bicycle Deck

The Ace of Spades in a Bicycle card deck has special branding.

Asimzb Edit By Jfitch, CC BY 3.0 <https://creativecommons.org/licenses/by/3.0>, via Wikimedia Commons: https://commons.wikimedia.org/wiki/File:Playing_cards-Edit1.jpg

The Bicycle Playing Cards are made by the United States Printing Company, with the first decks ever printed in 1885. The deck is called "Bicycle" because of the back design on the first issue, which displayed penny-farthings. If you're wondering what "penny-farthings" are, they're an early type of bicycle with high wheels at the front and small wheels at the back. They were also known as ordinary high-wheelers or high wheels.

But, back to the matter of the Bicycle deck. It has 52 cards, reds, and blacks, belonging to any of the four classical suits. The numbers go from 2 to 10 and end with the Jack card. The Ace of Spades has the Bicycle branding on it. Usually, this deck has poker hand ranks, 2 Jokers, and an informational card. For the most part, custom Bicycle cards have 2 extra cards along with the Jokers, which magicians use for tricks or advertising.

Gypsy Witch Deck

The Gypsy Witch Deck.
Photo de Esteban López sur Unsplash

The Gypsy Witch Fortune Telling Playing Cards were first published in 1904, and they're still being used today. They're older than the common Rider-Waite deck, which would first be published 5 years later. This deck is fascinating because it is inspired by Madam Lenormand herself. If you do your homework, you'll find many decks crafted in line with Lenormand's ideas, using mnemonic pictures on the cards. For some reason, these pictures and their interpretations don't align with the generally accepted interpretations of the suits or their numbers. These cards are also known as oracle cards and are a copy of the decks that came out after Lenormand died.

This deck comprises the same cards you'd find in a standard deck, except each card has a picture and interpretation. The images are reminiscent of the Victorian era, with the illustration style of the time making the cards even more interesting than other decks. Since the cards are already interpreted, and the meanings are right on them for you to read, you may assume that it would be easy to work with them since you don't have to memorize the interpretations, but that's not the case. Usually, in cartomancy, the suits have specific meanings.

For instance, the Hearts are about matters of the heart and other emotions. The Diamonds are about money and finances, and so on. However, with the Gypsy Witch Deck, you can't find any correlation between the pips and numbers and the images or interpretations. For instance, the 10 of Diamonds has a picture of a scythe and a bale of hay, and the interpretation reads, "The Scythe presages disappointment and when near the coffin, early death." Finding the correlation between that interpretation and the idea of Diamonds is pretty confusing.

Lenormand Deck

Lenormand cards are more practical in cartomancy.

The Lenormand deck is like Tarot in that it's used in cartomancy, but that's about it in terms of similarities. The Lenormand is much more practical because it's not about the impressions you get from looking at each one and is more about what goes on in your daily life. In other words, this deck is excellent when you want insight into practical affairs. Where Tarot is about the *why*, Lenormand is about the *how*; this deck has 36 cards, and it's the best option if you'd rather have clarity from your readings, especially when you draw the cards in pairs rather than singles. When you work with these alongside Tarot interpretations, you'd be hard-pressed to find any better way to find clarity in cartomancy.

Fin de Siècle Kipper

The new iteration of Kipper cards depicts important life events.

Tcg8888, CC BY-SA 4.0 <https://creativecommons.org/licenses/by-sa/4.0>, via Wikimedia Commons: https://commons.wikimedia.org/wiki/File:Kipper_Cards.jpg

Kipper cards are common in Germany and, similar to the Lenormand, have been in use since the mid-19th century. A new iteration of this Kipper deck is that by Ciro Marchetti, which is elegant in its presentation. This deck has 36 cards depicting essential life events and situations that most people find relatable, like being ill, taking a trip, working, getting married, etc. This deck is direct and easy to interpret, so even if you're new to cartomancy, you should have no problem figuring out what the cards mean. For instance, you have the High Honors card, which shows the King bestowing honor on a man kneeling before him. Or there's the marriage card, with a man and a woman dressed in wedding outfits.

To read Kipper cards, you can draw single cards. Usually, they're read in a straight line, and an odd number of cards is drawn (typically five or seven). It's also important to note the placement of the cards and how close they are to each other on the line, as these factors affect the reading. You also have to pay attention to the direction. Say, for instance, you draw the Gift card, and it's before the Main Male card. That could mean the man will get a gift. However, if the Gift card comes after the Main Male card, it could mean the man himself is offering someone else the gift. You read oracle and Tarot decks using intuition and interpret Lenormand cards metaphorically. However, Kipper cards are to be interpreted literally.

These are just a few of the decks you can use for divination. However, you should never forget that you can choose any other design or deck you want. It all comes down to your goals, preferences, and personal interests. Whether you prefer smaller or larger cards, more or fewer cards in your decks, or more or less flexibility in interpreting your cards, you should go with whatever resonates with you.

Choosing Your Deck

When choosing your deck, you must settle on something you're happy with. This means working with your intuition rather than choosing the first or only available deck you see. Here are some helpful tips to guide you.

First, you need to think about what you prefer. Everyone is different regarding the sort of symbolism and imagery they resonate with. Consider whether you'd rather have something more traditional or classic, like the Rider-Waite deck, for instance, or something more modern. Besides just the designs, consider what you want to accomplish with the deck. Do you want the kind that gives you straightforward interpretations? Or would you prefer something that is layered in meaning? These are questions you need to ask yourself as you make your choice.

Next, you need to do your homework. As you now know, different decks have different features. You need to think about what works best for you, but not only that, you should seek out others' opinions as well. For instance, check out fora and threads on cartomancy on Reddit, or look at the various reviews for each sort of deck. Also, look up the images of the deck's cards first to know if you'd be happy working with them. If you're still confused about which to choose, looking into the history of the decks may also help you figure out what works for you.

Now, you've got to interview the cards. Scratching your head at this one? That's understandable, but it shouldn't be strange. If the cards can tell you something about what to expect in life, there's no reason they can't tell you whether or not you'll work well with them! Therefore, you need to interview the deck before you settle on it. This means you need to ask it questions and then draw some cards to answer them. During this interview, your job is to observe how the deck offers you answers because, believe it or not, each deck has a unique personality. Just as certain personalities blend well together while others clash, one or the other scenario may occur with you and your cards.

How do you interview cards? Make them fill out a questionnaire or something? What you need to do is shuffle the cards. At the same time, you set your intention firmly in your mind; to become familiar with the deck's personality. When you've finished shuffling, it's time for your questions. Here are some of the things you could ask:

- What's your usual energy?
- What are the good things about you?
- What do you intend to do during readings?
- What do you have to teach me, if anything?
- What's the best way to work with each other?

With each question you ask, you should draw a card. Don't be in a hurry to interpret what each card means. Take your time and allow the answer to bubble up within you from your intuition. This way, you'll have an accurate grasp of the cards' energy and learn whether that's the deck you want to work with. This is just one way you can select or connect with a deck. There are other ways. For instance, you could:

1. **Spend some time with the deck.** The more you study each card and its symbolism, the more familiar it should become, and the better you can tell if it works for you. Shuffle the cards, handle them, and touch each one; their energy should connect with yours.

2. **Meditate with the deck of cards in your hands.** By meditating, you establish a connection with the cards on a profound level. If you like, you can bring the cards up to your heart energy center or chakra to feel their energy even better as you meditate. Also, the heart's intelligence will tell you immediately whether these cards are for you.

3. **Put the deck beneath your pillow** as you go to bed at night to get a sense of their energy. You can do this for several nights and pay particular attention to your dreams and how you feel when you wake up. When you sleep, your conscious mind goes offline. Your subconscious can pick up on subtle energies you miss at this time, carrying that information to you in your dreams or causing it to bubble up to your conscious mind when you awaken in the morning. Sleep is an excellent way to choose your deck.

4. **Draw your cards every day.** By doing this, you connect with the deck's energy, and you can observe how well the answers from the cards match your daily experiences.

Handling Your Deck

You need to be mindful of how you handle your deck, not just because you must keep them carefully but also because you must keep the energies pure during the reading. So, first of all, you must clear the deck of the energies from previous readings and any residual energies from anyone else who may have held the cards. Here are some ways you can clear the deck:

1. Shuffle the cards. The more thoroughly you shuffle them, the better the energy-clearing process.

2. Knock on the cards with your knuckles. Doing this will shake loose any old, stale energy lingering on the deck.

3. Smudge the deck. This means burning herbs like sage or palo santo and passing the cards through the smoke to eliminate negative and stale energies.

4. Finally, you can use visualization. Imagine a powerful golden light emanating from the palms of your hands and surrounding the deck, burning away any energy that doesn't belong there.

Maintaining and Protecting Your Cards

Keep the following in mind, and you'll have great-looking cards for a long time:

1. You need to treat your cards carefully so you don't damage them. Usually, the paper they're printed on is delicate, so you can't afford to be careless with them. Never crease the cards or bend them because that will not only not look good but will make it hard to shuffle them.

2. Do your best to wash and dry your hands before you handle the cards. If oil, dirt, or other things get on your cards, it's not a good look. Inevitably, your cards will get stained despite your best intentions. In this case, remove the stain using a soft, gentle wipe.

3. Put the cards away where they belong when you've finished. Keep them in a pouch or a box when you aren't working with them. Also, don't let them suffer from the effects of humidity or extreme temperatures.

4. Finally, respect your cards. They're tools that allow you to communicate with divinity, so you should treat them with reverence. This has the added benefit of giving you more effective results when you work with them. Always be mindful and intentional in your dealings with the cards, and you'll find that they work with you, not against you, all the time.

Now you've learned about various decks and how to care for them, what are the deeper meanings of the cards? How can you know for sure what they're saying to you? Find out about this and more in the following chapter.

Chapter Three: Symbolism and Meanings

Regardless of the deck you work with or the card you're looking at, there's much symbolism surrounding cartomancy. This symbolism has lasted for centuries. In this chapter, you will discover the traditional meanings of each card, suit, and number. You'll discover what the court cards are about and the esoteric meanings inherent in every deck. As you read, remember that each card's interpretation and meaning can change depending on the context and reader.

The Four Suits

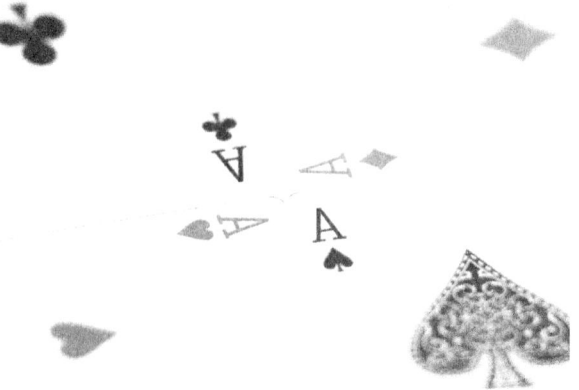

The four suits represent the four seasons in the year.
https://unsplash.com/photos/_MuYSOlPcWc

The four suits represent the four seasons in a year. Hearts represent spring, which is when you experience new growth. Diamonds represent the abundance and prosperity of the summer, and Clubs are reminiscent of autumn when you reap what you've sown. Spades are winter, a time when everything hibernates and goes within.

These suits are also connected to the four classical elements. The Hearts are connected to watery emotions and the deep wells of intuition within you. Diamonds are of the earth, pregnant with resources and rich with treasures. Clubs are connected to flames of creativity and passion that burn in one and all, even though they are but embers in some and in others a raging inferno. As for Spades, they are airy cards that have to do with intellect, mental prowess, and communication.

The Hearts

The Hearts suit is also known as the Cups suit in Tarot. It's one of the four main suits you'll encounter in cartomancy, and it's all about matters of the heart, dreams, relationships, emotions, intuition, and the subconscious or unconscious. It's about the things that bubble beneath the surface of the deep. It is believed that the physical world isn't the only one, and it shares a connection with invisible realms, realms you'd consider spiritual or metaphysical. The archetypes and symbols on the Hearts suit are connected to those realms, possessing deep insight into what it means to be alive and evolve spiritually.

The Hearts suit is the suit that tells you everything about the relationships in your life and how they influence you. It tells you about your spiritual path and how you're doing with your self-exploration and discovery. The cards in this suit will reveal everything about your challenges and victories, and the things you have experienced or will experience that will change you for better or worse as you discover your authentic, spiritual self. This suit represents messages from your intuitive self and wisdom that wells up from the subconscious mind. It's about getting in touch with worlds unseen, following your instincts, feeling your gut on every issue, and trusting what it tells you.

Hearts are connected to the heart itself, which, as everyone knows, is the center of love, passion, hate, and other emotions. The heart is at the center of who you are. It's from your heart that your true desires are born and where you hold your true self, devoid of any of the ego's decorations, masks, and costumes. Therefore, The Heart suit is an invitation to your emotional world, asking you to dive deep and receive the valuable treasures in your heart's wisdom. Here's a quick look at what each card in this suit implies.

Ace of Hearts: Expect a new beginning in relationships and friendships. This could be a new lover, marriage, or something good happening to you. It represents the potential to develop powerful emotional ties with others.

2 of Hearts: This card represents the connection of two people as they become one in love. It's also asking you to spend some time with those you love. This card carries the energy of balance, connection, harmony, and partnership, representing the ideas of emotional cooperation and compatibility. It's asking you to demonstrate more understanding as you relate with others, which means being open to vulnerability and reconciliation.

3 of Hearts: When you draw this card, it indicates that you aren't very committed to a relationship, or at the very least, you feel indecisive about it. However, some interpret this more positively. As they say, it represents an abundant, joyful experience of love in every way possible.

4 of Hearts: Emotional stability and security are the energies that this card exudes. It tells you that you're in a committed partnership or marriage. When about home affairs, it implies that you're in a safe and nurturing environment. The 4 of Hearts is also about learning to set boundaries and ground your emotions to continue to enjoy the love that feels safe.

5 of Hearts: Drawing this card represents enormous changes that will affect your family and home life. These changes could be good or bad. Perhaps someone's getting divorced or moving to a new place. Either way, the status quo will be disrupted. The 5 of Hearts is the heartbreak card, representing grief, loss, release, and resilience when dealing with emotional turbulence.

6 of Hearts: Expect harmonious interactions with others, leading you to whatever you desire. This card is about freely giving and receiving love and letting kindness lead the way in your dealings with others. Its energy is forgiving and selfless.

7 of Hearts: This card can represent someone likely to disappoint you. Alternatively, it represents being introspective and searching your heart to discover your true feelings about someone or something.

8 of Hearts: Commitment, developing stronger bonds, and emotional changes are the messages this card carries. It's about sticking with someone or something for the long haul, being mature in expressing your emotions, choosing loyalty above anything else, and investing everything you can to develop and sustain loving connections in your life. Drawing this card means you'll be at an event that will give you the opportunity of a lifetime, romantically or financially.

9 of Hearts: This card tells you someone wants to take their relationship with you to greater heights. Perhaps they'd like to propose or start a family with you. Expect to experience satisfaction in your connections and love affairs.

10 of Hearts: Expect some good news. You'll learn of this at a party or someplace where many people are gathered. The card also represents family unity and being fulfilled emotionally in that context.

Jack of Hearts: This card represents your most trusted friend or lover. When you draw this along with the Queen of Hearts, it could represent a couple. On its own, it's someone creative, sensitive, and full of compassion. Usually, it represents a young person. This card also represents your insights from intuition and emotional development.

Queen of Hearts: This card represents your fantasy. It could also stand in for a female lover or someone pregnant. Marriage may also be on the horizon. This card's energy is nurturing, deep, and intuitive. It's the embodiment of femininity.

King of Hearts: The King of Hearts represents masculine energy and can stand in for a father figure. It's a man of influence who is in touch with his emotions and is sweet. This person demonstrates love in the context of leadership, balancing his authority with his emotions so that he tempers justice with kindness.

The Diamonds

Sometimes the Diamonds suit is called the Coins or Pentacles suit. This suit concerns practical affairs, money, material wealth, and the physical world. The Diamonds are about everything you own, your career, and what you do to advance in life. The Diamonds represent everything about manifestation and making your dreams come true. They show you all the practical things you must do to get where you need to go, how much effort will be required to make your goals happen, and whether you should keep treading the path you're on.

Diamonds demonstrate what you need to do to help you get in the flow of prosperity and abundance using practical skills that you possess and resources around you that you may have been blind to for a while.

It's about your business and vocation and guidance on what to do to get the financial status you desire. It's about taking your dreams and making them real through action.

Esoterically, the Diamonds suit also has to do with your health. It's about how good you feel in your body and what you can do to take better care of it. The cards in this suit can show you the connection between your spiritual life and your health, so you know the importance of feeding yourself on both levels so you can be the best version of yourself.

Finally, this suit is about integrating your spiritual and physical lives. It's about ensuring that the things you hold in high esteem align with what you're experiencing in the observable, objective world to feel like you have a purpose and meaning in your life. These cards ask you to remember that your physical life should be a tool to help you develop spiritually. The Diamonds are connected to the diamond itself. This hard, durable thing represents strength, endurance, and resilience. Think about forming a diamond; you can draw parallels from that process to your life. To produce the precious stone, there's got to be some refinement, and this is the same with your life. You need to take the raw materials you've been given — your talents, skills, and natural inclinations — and make them work for you, and this is what Diamonds generally teach you when you draw them. Now, let's see what each card means in this suit.

Ace of Diamonds: Drawing this card means there's something important that you will learn about your business. It's a sign that there's potential for you to make something of yourself financially or that abundance is coming your way. The message here is that you should prepare yourself for financial prosperity and other opportunities for growth in a material sense, so you can experience stability in that aspect of life.

2 of Diamonds: When you spot this card, expect to receive some good news about your investments. The number two represents the idea of duality and balance, so drawing this card means you must find a balance between your material pursuits and spiritual growth. It implies that you should find balance in allocating and using your resources.

3 of Diamonds: The 3 of Diamonds card demonstrates some uncertainty regarding finances. If you're not careful, you may be caught in legal problems. Alternatively, this card represents manifesting your abundance at last, working with your practical skills, and improving your craft. This card tells you that you have talents you must develop and work hard at, as this is how you will gain the prosperity you seek.

4 of Diamonds: Drawing this card means you need to be more responsible with your finances to stay stable. It's about accumulating immense wealth through making sensible, smart choices and working hard on your goals.

5 of Diamonds: You should expect some sort of economic change. It could be good or bad, but whatever it is, it definitely requires preparation. You may have to contend with financial setbacks or have a sudden windfall. The best way to tell what it might be is within the context of other cards. Drawing this card implies you've got to be resourceful and creative in handling the situation.

6 of Diamonds: It's time to pay attention to your debts. Do your best to settle them. Also, look at your budget and adjust it or create one if you don't have one. You also should look into investing for your financial future. The 6 of Diamonds is also a card of generosity, blessings, giving, and receiving. It tells you that the more you give, the more you receive.

7 of Diamonds: Be mindful of what you do with your money, especially regarding investment. You must evaluate your options carefully before you make a decision. Be prudent about what you do with your resources. Think about where you're at financially before making a major decision or putting your money into something.

8 of Diamonds: Drawing this card is lovely because a great, unexpected windfall is just around the corner. The number 8 is reminiscent of the infinity sign, and you can expect a good amount of money that is impactful enough to feel like infinite abundance. Keep your eyes on the prize and stay dedicated to your goal, even if it seems impossible.

9 of Diamonds: This card tells you that you've attained or are close to attaining fulfillment in your financial endeavors. The number nine represents completions and endings; therefore, this card could also represent the idea of finishing a financial journey you've been on, having finally attained security. It's the card of the materialization of everything you've ever wanted to attain relative to your finances and business.

10 of Diamonds: You're drawing close to the very zenith of your accomplishments. You've worked hard and will now enjoy the fruits of your labor. You will be greatly rewarded for choosing the best, most balanced path to success.

Jack of Diamonds: This card represents someone full of ambition. This practical person diligently applies himself to his work, keeping his career goals within sight. This person could be male or female and is driven to get things started and succeed at entrepreneurship. This person is also young (usually). Some, however, say that the Jack of Diamonds represents someone bringing you bad financial news. You can tell which is the case by working within the context of the other cards you've drawn (or will draw) and the question being answered.

Queen of Diamonds: This represents a woman or feminine force with a love for parties and gossip. You may think of this card as someone who is abundant, practical, and has much wisdom to share with you when it comes to finances. The card is about being financially independent and prudent with your money so that you grow it even more.

King of Diamonds: This card can represent a businessman (or a businesswoman with masculine energy) who has found great power and success in his affairs. This person is in charge of wealth and is a responsible decision-maker. The card represents your power to create abundance for yourself, dominate finance, and manage your resources with great wisdom.

The Clubs

Sometimes, the Clubs suit is known as the Baton or Wands suit. Its energy is a representation of the fire of creativity and inspiration. This suit is connected to your growth, passion, and ambition. It is about starting new endeavors. It is about the spark of inspiration that you get to begin something new. Whenever you draw a card from the Club suit, it represents giving birth to new ideas and nurturing those ideas so that they blossom into their fullness.

The Club Suit is about discovering yourself and developing your spiritual awareness to the point where you can use it to influence your physical life. The cards you draw from this suit all offer guidance that aligns with your inspiration. In other words, all the wisdom you receive from these cards is rooted in spiritual principles that govern life.

The Clubs are all about your passion and determination to be a success. It is about expressing your highest calling as a leader and choosing the attitude of determination when you embark on any creative endeavor. Clubs carry the energy of taking charge in asserting your authentic self. Often, when people draw this card, they are required to express their inner strength when dealing with challenges in life.

The Club suit is also connected to intuition. It is about waking up your latent psychic abilities and using them following divine wisdom to bring you the spiritual insight and physical changes that you desire. Clubs ask you to trust the voice from within because it is the voice of truth and transformational passion. Therefore, the Club suit is all about alchemy, taking the raw material of the passion within you and converting that into the manifestation you seek. Now it's time to examine what each card in the Clubs' suit represents.

Ace of Clubs: This represents a desire to know everything you can. It can also represent a unique skill or talent that you alone possess. This card is the essence of fire. It is about the creative energy that you use for new ideas. Drawing this card means you're about to start something new along creative lines or spiritual lines about which you are passionate.

2 of Clubs: This card is about cooperation and blending your ideas with others. It is about acknowledging the creative forces within you and someone else and finding a way to bring them together that works. This card is also a reminder that you need to communicate clearly and sincerely with others and do your best not to get entangled in confrontations to avoid getting into a situation where you are disappointed.

3 of Clubs: When you draw this card, it represents either an extreme amount of creativity (which is a good thing) or the stress you must undergo in creating something. The three Clubs also represent the ideas of expansion and growth and the realization that you can create much more than you thought possible. When you draw this card, it asks you to look within and discover your skills and do your best to develop them. As you do this, opportunities will present themselves to you, allowing you to broaden your horizons and achieve much more than you thought possible. This card also asks you to be enthusiastic and optimistic about the new things that come your way and be willing to try things outside your comfort zone.

4 of Clubs: Find a way to ground your creative energy. In other words, you are meant to find practical outlets for that energy to convert potential into something real. The 4 of Clubs is about foundation, stability, and having a solid framework for your ideas. It is about going after your creative goals for the long term. Drawing this card also means that you must do your best to cultivate a stable sense of self and peace of mind to experience something amazing.

5 of Clubs: You need to change something about your life. It's a good time to discover new things. You may be pleasantly surprised to find you have an affinity for a sport or hobby you never thought you'd be interested in. Expect to contend with conflicts and challenges as you express yourself creatively. To overcome these challenges, you must be flexible and willing to change. Seek innovative ways to fix your problems. Being resilient and persevering through everything will help you.

6 of Clubs: This is a card of success and victory in your creative endeavors. You will be or are being recognized for all that you have achieved in the field of creativity. It results from all the work you have put into obtaining your goals and everyone finally recognizing your creative prowess. This card affirms that you are a creative powerhouse and must lean on your intuition to gain better things.

7 of Clubs: You feel stuck, trapped, or confined. This could be not just in your creative life but your romantic life. You need to take time to be introspective. Reflect on your life so far, and explore yourself –that is how you will grow. You must seek guidance from within and ensure that whatever creative projects you are involved in align with your true values.

8 of Clubs: The energy of this card is progress. It is about the momentum you experience as you work to accomplish your creative goals. You will manifest the visions you have held in your mind as you are driven toward success. Drawing this card means you must focus and stay determined as you pursue your dreams. Some readers say that this card is also a sign that you are struggling with confusion. They say it means you must be careful because you may experience major problems relating to others if you do not sort out your problem.

9 of Clubs: 9, the number of completion, implies that this card is about finishing a phase or project. You have finally achieved the dreams that you sought. The satisfaction that you have sought for the longest time is now yours.

10 of Clubs: This card says you will be traveling soon. Your travels are essential to your creative endeavors. Therefore, do not be tempted to pass on an opportunity to go somewhere new. This card also represents blending what you know and have experienced to apply that to your creative work.

Jack of Clubs: The Jack of Clubs is someone you can trust. This is an honest person who makes a point of telling you everything that you must know. This person may be a close friend of yours.

Queen of Clubs: The Queen of Clubs is a woman full of charisma. She is in a position of power. She can help you with whatever you seek to learn or accomplish.

King of Clubs: This represents a man who never compromises when it comes to his integrity. This man is an excellent person to have by your side as a friend because he constantly proves himself to be loyal and generous.

The Spades

The Spades suit is also known as the Swords suit. This suit is all about obstacles and difficulties you must face. Very often, the suit is considered a negative one. It usually is about having to make very difficult choices and decisions in life about major things.

The Spades suit is about communication, sharing ideas, and intellect. It is connected to the idea of being rational and working with the power of your mind. The sword is often seen as a symbol representing discernment in making decisions. You can use it to cut through confusing clouded thoughts, so you can get to the heart and truth of the matter.

The cards in this suit are meant to help you to figure out the difference between what is real and what only appears to be real. Drawing cards from this suit will help you make informed decisions based on solid facts. This suit is also related to the power in your tongue, in the sense that you can give life or kill, depending on the words you choose when interacting with others. The Spades can help you figure out how to deal with sensitive issues and express yourself so that you deliver the truth without severely damaging someone.

Another thing about the Spades suit is that it will help you discover the limiting beliefs holding you back from achieving your highest ideals. If you know that you can stomach the truth about yourself, you will not shy away from any reading with a Spade in it. You will understand the power you can use for your benefit as it can help you to transmute conflicts and challenges into opportunities to improve in every way possible. Now that you understand what the Spades suit is all about, it is time to talk about the individual cards in this suit.

Ace of Spades: You will deal with major changes in your life. Something you've grown accustomed to will have to end to make room for the new. This card represents the fact that your mind has infinite potential and intellect.

2 of Spades: You're going to encounter a difficult situation. If improperly handled, this may lead you and a loved one to part ways. You must carefully consider your choices now, considering various viewpoints in order to make a balanced decision.

3 of Spades: You will be sad due to something stressful. You may receive terrible news. There's also a possibility that your job security may be threatened. Or, you may be dealing with fear and indecision regarding a certain matter. The Three of Spades is also about expanding your mind through learning, discovering the skills that you have within you, and following through on your ideas to see where they lead.

4 of Spades: You should expect your health or career to become stable soon. The tough times that you have been contending with or about to come to an end. This card is the energy of stability and organization regarding your intellectual pursuits. It asks you to be disciplined in your affairs.

5 of Spades: Very soon, you will have to walk away from something with which you have grown familiar. You may be leaving your job for a new one or relocating to a new home. You may also be dealing with the end of your romantic relationship. The 5 of Spades is a card that embodies the conflicts you must deal with in your mind when facing adversity. The card tells you that the storm is the opportunity for you to grow and become something more by tapping into your inner resilience.

6 of Spades: Expect to be rocked in your career or finances. This card also represents the path you must take from your present confused state to clarity. This card calls you out of your limited thinking to more expansive ideas.

7 of Spades: Soon, you may have to contend with losing someone important due to disagreements or other issues. In addition, the 7 of Spades ask you to look within yourself and question your beliefs to expand beyond the cage in which they have trapped you. This is a card of self-awareness.

8 of Spades: You may have to struggle with challenges at work. These challenges will force you to come to a point where you must make a critical decision about what to do next. This is the card of mental fortitude and determination. You will make your way through this obstacle one way or another.

9 of Spades: You may experience a loss due to death. This card also asks you to do what you must to set yourself free of negative thought patterns to end your life's current phase of hardship and move on to something newer and better.

10 of Spades: You will struggle with grief and worry. This could be because you're struggling with health issues or the aftermath of bad news.

You may also find that you are gripped by fear. It is important to understand that this is temporary.

Jack of Spades: This individual is extremely negative. If you are not careful, they will stab you in the back. They are also holding you back from accomplishing what you need to. Therefore, taking a critical look at the people in your life to pinpoint the toxic person and get rid of them as soon as possible is important.

Queen of Spades: This woman is an expert at manipulating others to get what she wants. Often, the results of her manipulation do not benefit anyone else besides her. You must beware of this character because she is extremely cruel and is constantly on the lookout to display her malevolence toward anyone within her sight.

King of Spades: This individual is a man who has authority and is in the habit of causing trouble wherever he is. You need to beware of this character because he will cause you trouble, particularly regarding your relationship.

Now that you understand what each card implies, you can also check in with your intuition to see what else you pick up on during a reading from the card. Remember that these are only guidelines and that their meanings can change drastically depending on the context in which the cards appear. The next chapter will reveal all you need to learn about spreads and layouts that you can use in cartomancy.

Chapter Four: Spreads and Lay-outs

In this chapter, you'll learn that there are various cartomancy methods. Ultimately, you're the one who gets to decide the technique and specific deck of cards to be used. In this chapter, you will learn about the most common, basic spreads and, later, the more complex ones.

The Basic Spreads

The following spreads are the most common ones and worth looking into before you dive into the more complex stuff.

The One-Card Draw

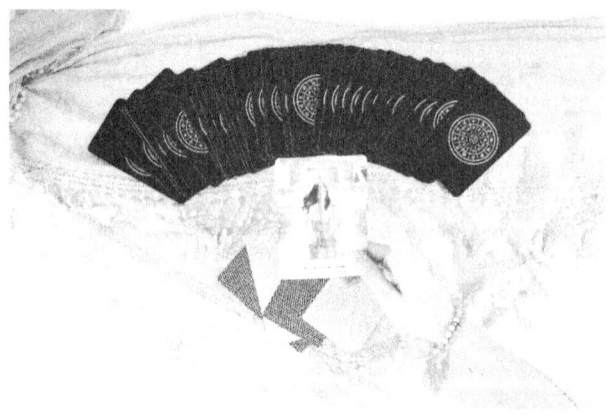

One-card draw.
https://unsplash.com/photos/QdmMWxQXJ2Y

This is one of the easiest draws you can use in your practice. All you have to do is draw one card out of the deck to respond to a specific question or gain insight into a particular problem you're dealing with. The beauty of this draw is that it is beginner-friendly, and you can gain profound insights from just one card.

To perform a one-card draw, you must first enter a meditative state by quieting your mind. Then, shuffle the deck while keeping your intention or question in mind. As you shuffle, you will get an intuitive nudge when it's time to stop and pick a card from the deck.

Once you've drawn the card, it's time to interpret its meaning. This means you need to pause to look at the card's colors, pictures, and any symbols it may have. You must understand that every card possesses a unique story seeking interpretation through the medium of your intuition. Therefore, you should take your time with this and not be in a hurry to say something. If you have trouble understanding what the card is trying to tell you, do not be afraid to draw another card (though this would not be the one-card draw when you do so).

One of the major advantages of working with this one-card draw is that it is simple enough to establish a deep connection to the cards you draw. When you are focused on just one card, it becomes easier for you to learn to work with your intuition and better interpret the meaning of each card presented, depending on the context. The one-card draw is the best option when you don't have enough time or are in a hurry.

As great as this draw is, you must realize that it does not offer a broad enough perspective on your question or situation compared to the more complex spreads. This is because you glean information from just one card rather than several. However, this doesn't mean you should snub the one-card draw method, as it can still give you the most profound answers.

The Three-Card Spread

The three-card spread.

As you've already gathered from the name of the spread, the three-card spread is one where you draw three cards out of the deck and set them up in a specific pattern to indicate certain things. There are several iterations of the three-card spread. Let's take a look at each one.

Past — Present — Future: This is a classic method of working with a three-card spread that lets you know the circumstances and influences surrounding your current location. The first card is your past and lets you know how you got to where you are. The second card represents your present and demonstrates exactly what you face regarding challenges and opportunities. The final card shows you what the future could hold. It allows you to see possible outcomes if you continue your path.

Mind — Body — Spirit: This spread will show you what's happening within yourself on different levels. The first card drawn represents your mind. It's meant to show you the thoughts that you have consciously and beneath the surface, what you believe in, and your academic goals. The second card is representative of your body. This card shows you the state of your health and well-being and other important information about your physical self. The final card drawn represents your spirit, giving you insights into the path you walk spiritually, how you can grow, and how you can rely on your intuition to become an evolved being.

Problem — Action — Outcome: Working with this technique, the first card represents the obstacle or problem you're dealing with. It shows you its true source so that you can address it at its core. The next card is the action you should take to fix whatever is broken. The last card is the result or outcome you should expect if you follow the recommended action path.

The great thing about the three-card spread is that it's also a simple one for beginners. Better than the one-card draw, this method gives you a more comprehensive understanding of the question. Working with elements such as your past, present, and future gives you a deep, holistic perspective of your present situation. This implies that you can make choices from enough data based on truth, and you will feel more comfortable and confident in pursuing your path.

As great as a three-card spread is, it does have some limitations. For instance, this card spread may not be adequate for digging into the complex, intricate nature of certain circumstances where you may need more insight. It offers a snapshot of things rather than getting heavily into the situation. Another thing you need to be aware of: the meaning of each card may be taken out of context if you do not consider the three cards as a unit. Therefore, you need to consider how each card interacts with the others before you offer your reading.

The Celtic Cross Spread

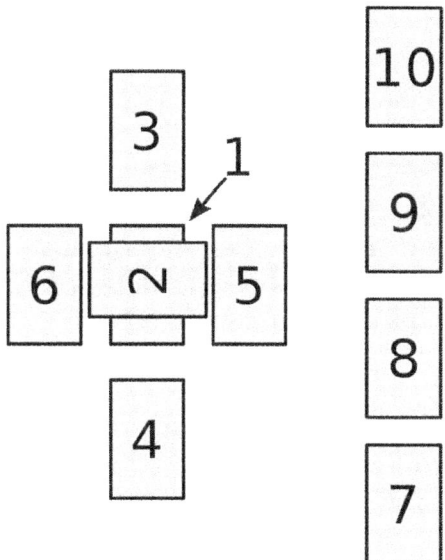

The Celtic cross spread.
WolfgangRieger. CC0, via Wikimedia Commons:
https://commons.wikimedia.org/wiki/File:Celtic_Cross_Spread_-_Waite.svg

The Celtic cross spread is an interesting spread with 10 cards set up to form a cross and staff. The first known mention of the Celtic cross spread was in 1910 by A. E. Waite in the introduction to A Pictorial Key to the Tarot. Waite was part of the Hermetic Order of the Golden

Dawn, which often used this specific spread. There are various ways to do the Celtic cross spread.

The Traditional Celtic Cross: With this spread, 10 cards are set out in the cross pattern. The first card represents the issue on which you want clarity. It talks about the main theme of the question being posed. The second card represents the forces that influence the situation you are contending with and the challenges you must face. The third card is your subconscious mind, and it's meant to help you learn the underlying factors in that situation and the hidden motivations of all the players involved. The fourth card represents your very recent past. It tells you all you need to know about what led you to where you are.

The fifth card represents a possible future result or the energies coming into play. The sixth card is your immediate future and offers information about what to expect in the coming days or weeks. The seventh card represents you. It shows you your attitude towards the circumstance you're faced with and how you are addressing it. The eighth card is representative of the external forces like events and people that will have a part to play in the final outcome. The 9th card sheds light on your dreams, fears, and hopes. It helps you understand what's going on with you emotionally. The final card is the ultimate resolution or result of the situation.

The Modified Celtic Cross: This version differs from the traditional one in that extra cards help you gain more insight into the situation. It starts as the traditional spread, but after those 10 classic cards, you can draw more cards to place in certain positions to gain more information or clarity on those aspects. For instance, you may want more information on the fifth card to understand the possible outcomes of the problem you're dealing with and be better prepared to handle them, so you can draw another card from the deck to clarify that fifth one. The great thing about these extra cards is that they make your reading more nuanced and in-depth, providing a more satisfactory answer you can act on confidently.

The wonderful thing about the Celtic cross spread, whether the traditional or modified version, is that you can use it to not just look at your past, present, and future but to understand everything that's going on, on a conscious and subconscious level. It's a flexible cartomancy spread because it can address all aspects of your life, like personal growth, love life, finances, etc. When you lay out all the cards in a Celtic cross spread, you are presented with the smorgasbord of symbolism that provides a much richer, layered, detailed interpretation of events.

As great as this spread is, it does have certain drawbacks. For one thing, it may be too complex for some people. It does require an in-depth understanding of the interplay between cards and how their meanings affect one another. So, as a new practitioner of cartomancy, you need to grasp what each card means and get familiar with how these meanings can influence one another before you begin working with this spread. You will encounter challenges when it comes to interpreting the cards. Still, if you choose to be patient, work with your intuition, and continue to practice, you will find yourself getting more adept at working with the Celtic cross spread.

The Grand Tableau

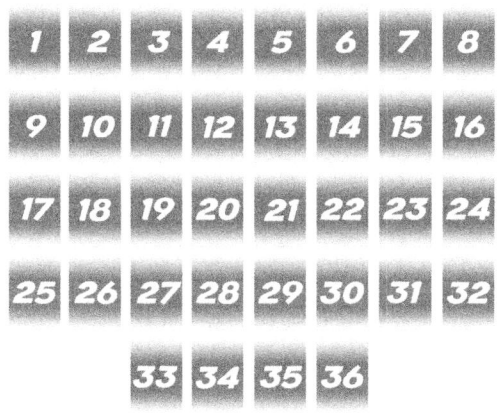

Grand Tableau Layout

Using all 36 cards in the deck, lay out the cards in the order shown above
4 rows of 8 cards
1 row of 4 cards

The Grand Tableau spread

The Grand Tableau is a spread that requires the Lenormand deck. Grand Tableau is French, meaning "big picture." The lovely thing about the spread is that it'll give you a panoramic view of everything in your life, from the past to your present and future. There are various ways that you can use the Grand Tableau spread.

The Traditional Grand Tableau: In this spread, you will lay 36 cards in a particular pattern to form a grid. Every card has its position that stands for the various aspects of your life or the question you're asking. Usually, the layout has various rows and columns, and they all intersect to create new meaning. The various positions can have different meanings depending on the system of interpretation that you follow.

The Focused Question Grand Tableau: This variation of the Grand Tableau spread focuses on just one area of your life or one question. You work with all 36 cards. However, the advantage of this version of the Grand Tableau is that it will allow you to concentrate on the cards specifically connected to your inquiry. When you pay specific attention to the intersections or key spots tied to your question, you can gain profound wisdom about that area of your life.

The Grand Tableau is another spread offering you a deep, comprehensive insight into your situation. The level of nuance and detail you can attain with this spread is amazing and very useful. This is also an excellent spread for forecasting your possible future. Of course, this is not without its drawbacks, as it is a rather complex spread, and it requires a lot of time and focus to interpret this correctly.

The Tree of Life Spread

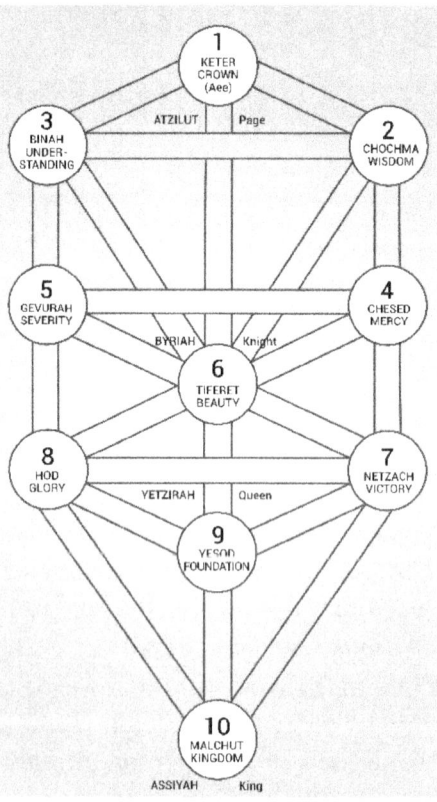

The Tree of Life spread.

This spread is rooted in ancient Kabbalistic wisdom. It is inspired by the Tree of Life in the Kabbalah. There are various ways you can use the spread.

The Traditional Tree of Life Spread: The cards are set out to mimic the Tree of Life in the Kabbalah. There are 10 positions in this layout, each representing one emanation or sephira on the tree. The cards are laid down from top to bottom, and each emanation connects to a specific aspect of life. The first card addresses spirituality and represents what you believe in and practice in your spiritual life and your connection to the divine. The next card is the persona card, which gives insight into how you appear in other people's eyes. The next card is the subconscious card. This card will expose what you truly feel, desire, and think beneath the surface. After this card is the home and family card, which shows you what life is like with your family members. The next one demonstrates your connection to your ancestors, as well as the history of your family. The sixth card represents how your past has played out and how it affects your present reality. The seventh card demonstrates your connection to other realms, like the spirit world. The eighth card of wisdom shows all the insights you have gained through your life experience. The ninth card is a card that shows how you have grown and developed or how you will do so in the future. The final card is the outcome card that demonstrates the likely results of the circumstance you are dealing with if you continue on the path of action you have chosen.

The Modified Tree of Life Spread: This spread has been modified in such a way as to offer more flexibility in the reading of the cards. You may assign certain areas of your life to specific positions on the Tree of Life that tie into the matter about which you are asking questions. You could pay attention only to matters involving your career, love life, or anything else.

Romany Tarot Spread

1-7. **Past.** 8-14. **Present.** 15-21. **Future.**

The Romany spread

This spread requires 21 cards set up in three rows with seven cards per row. It is also known as the Gypsy spread.

The Traditional Romany Spread: Each row represents an aspect of your existence in this spread. The first represents the past, the second represents the present, and the last represents the future. The cards are read sequentially to gain insight into all the influences affecting your life.

The Modified Romany Spread: This one is similar to the traditional one, except you can customize it to your needs. For instance, you may add cards or remove cards. You can add extra rows if they serve your purpose or adjust the layout so that you only focus on specific aspects of life that may not necessarily correlate to the traditional past, present, or future setup.

Now that you understand the various spreads and layouts that you can use in cartomancy, the question is, how do you accurately interpret combined cards? Also, what does it mean when a card shows up reversed? You will discover the answers to these questions in the following chapter.

Chapter Five: Combinations and Reversed Cards

When reading multiple cards, it is important to understand that they will always influence the overall meaning you get from your reading. This is because the energies of the cards interact with one another in unique ways, varying from context to context. In this chapter, you'll learn how to interpret multiple cards that show up in a layout or spread and understand the reversed cards that definitely will turn up.

Patterns can be found when reading multiple cards.
https://unsplash.com/photos/dttmeqFUDSU

Finding Patterns

Seeking patterns in the various combinations of cards you draw can add more dimension and depth to your readings. It's common to look for patterns in pairs, trios, or quartets, so you can discover the underlying connections and other hidden meanings that aren't immediately easy to glean.

Pairs: The first pattern to consider is known as the pair. This is when you have two cards with similar numbers or suits showing up with each other side by side. Following are some keyword interpretations of the various pairs you may encounter. Still, please note that you should also work with your intuition because that could offer something more nuanced in your interpretations or even different from what you have read in this book.

- **Pair of Aces:** Reconnection
- **Pair of Kings:** Helpful advice
- **Pair of Queens:** Expressing curiosity
- **Pair of Jacks:** Having discussions
- **Pair of Tens:** New luck
- **Pair of Nines:** Upcoming contentment and satisfaction
- **Pair of Eights:** Instability
- **Pair of Sevens:** Love shared
- **Pair of Sixes:** Contrasts and differences
- **Pair of Fives:** Insecurity
- **Pair of Fours:** Small opportunities
- **Pair of Threes:** Making choices
- **Pair of Twos:** Separation

Pair of Jokers: Anything can happen **Trios:** These patterns show up in threes. The following are the interpretations of each trio:

- **Trio of Aces:** Harmony and balance
- **Trio of Kings:** Excellent support
- **Trio of Queens:** Gossip
- **Trio of Jacks:** Quarrelsome energy
- **Trio of Tens:** Recompense
- **Trio of Nines:** Success

- **Trio of Eights:** Lightened load
- **Trio of Sevens:** Accomplishment and fulfillment
- **Trio of Sixes:** Dedication and hard work
- **Trio of Fives:** Satisfaction
- **Trio of Fours:** High odds of success
- **Trio of Threes:** Balance and stability
- **Trio of Twos:** Switching lanes

Quartets: There are four suits, so naturally, you can expect interesting quartets to show up in readings occasionally. Here are keyword interpretations of quartets to guide you:

- **Quartet of Aces:** Victory
- **Quartet of Kings:** Success, acknowledgment, and honor
- **Quartet of Queens:** Scandalous events
- **Quartet of Jacks:** Fighting and battling
- **Quartet of Tens:** Better changes
- **Quartet of Nines:** Sudden windfall and unexpected, good news
- **Quartet of Eights:** Worry and concern
- **Quartet of Sevens:** Sameness
- **Quartet of Sixes:** Sudden difficulties and curveballs
- **Quartet of Fives:** Joy and happiness
- **Quartet of Fours:** 50-50 odds
- **Quartet of Threes:** Optimism and hope
- **Quartet of Twos:** Being at an intersection, crossroads, and choices

Considering the Numbers

When interpreting drawn cards, you should consider what the numbers mean, as they will add more depth to the meaning you glean from them. Every number has unique energy and meaning, bringing you greater clarity when you understand them. You can also look at the numbers from the context of numerology, which is the study of the influence of numbers on everyone and every aspect of everyday life. Some cartomancers will assign each number two meanings, which are opposite. The positive meaning is applied when the number appears in a red suit. The negative interpretation is used instead if it's in the black suit. With that said, here's a look at the meanings of each number when working with this system:

- 1 — Beginning or ending; starting or finishing
- 2 — Working together or working against each other
- 3 — Increasing or reducing; expanding or contracting
- 4 — Stability or instability; balance or imbalance
- 5 — Action or rest
- 6 — Communication or silence; knowledge or ignorance
- 7 — Improving or regressing
- 8 — Health or illness; healing or deteriorating health
- 9 — Dreams or disappointments
- 10 — Victory or defeat; success or failure
- 11 (the Jack) — Thinking or speaking
- 12 (the Queen) — External guidance or internal wisdom
- 13 (the King) — Leading or following

Key Positions

As you look at the spread, you should pay attention to the positions of the cards, particularly the ones in the corners or the center. These cards are like foundations to your reading; their meaning will offer you deep insight that shapes the answers the reader seeks. The middle card is like the heart of your reading, demonstrating the main essence of the question. You cannot ignore this card because it represents everything happening here and now, which spreads its influence like tentacles into the future. When considering the cards in the middle, you should ask yourself questions. For instance, what does a card in the middle show you about the current situation in which you seek clarity? What's the connection of the middle card to the challenge you're facing or the main goal you want to accomplish? What message does this card convey regarding the most important aspects of your life? By looking at the card in the middle, focusing on it, and allowing your intuition to speak to you about it, you will develop a deep insight into the forces responsible for your destiny.

You must also consider the cards that show up at the corners. Usually, the corner cards are very important. Within these cards, you will find the keys to hidden doors in the subconscious that help to explain exactly what the seeker is going through and their deepest desires.

It is also important for you to consider the relationship between the cards as you read them. You will learn so many secrets by considering how close they are or how far apart and the alignments they share. For instance, when you have cards that face each other across your spread, these cards may act as mirrors to each other, representing opposing energies that seek balance. However, you notice that certain cards appear to oppose each other. In that case, you must ask yourself what that implies for your query. Sometimes, the cards will form a bridge between other cards. These cards are easy to pick out because you'll notice the same suit or number creating this bridge. It is important to pay attention to these things because they will show you how various elements dance with one another to create the show that is your life. They will offer much more minute detail than just considering individual cards independently.

As you observe your spread, you may realize that certain cards appear more prominent than others, drawing your eye. It appears as though their energy is literally screaming at you for attention. One of the ways to notice these cards is through their size or how closely placed they are to the center. You may also give significance to the cards based on their connection to the question that you were asking. Make a point of getting in touch with your intuition before doing the reading. You may feel the energetic, emotional pull of a card. It is important to pay attention to any card that draws your eye and allow it to dictate the main themes of the reading.

Elemental Associations

Another way you can glean meaning from the card is by considering the primal elements the cards and suits possess. By considering the interplay of the various elements that show up, you will understand the dynamics of the various cards and how they affect one another to give you an on-point reading.

As you already know, each suit has its own element. You can return to Chapter 3 to refresh your memory about each suit. When you understand the elemental energies contained in its suit, you can then take that information and use it to figure out what the various suit combinations in your reading may imply. For instance, when you notice that you have different suits acting in alignment, which suggests that the elements complement each other. For instance, you get Heart and Diamond cards in your reading. The Hearts are emotional cards, and the Diamonds are practical cards, and merging these two could indicate financial stability and consideration for your feelings while getting financial freedom.

It is also possible to have a clash of energies between the cards. For instance, the Club is a card that suggests fire and ambition. If you draw that card along with a Spade, which suggests being introspective, it could be a sign that you are having trouble finding the sweet spot between taking action and thinking something over. This means you have to find a way to balance these things.

Sometimes, you will discover that one suit appears to dominate your entire reading. This tells you that elemental energy is predominant in your life. Considering this, you can uncover clues that help you understand your life's work and theme. For instance, discovering that your reading is rife with Diamonds could mean you are heavily focused on the material side of life.

Another noteworthy thing you must consider is how balanced or imbalanced the reading is regarding elemental energy. For instance, when reading is properly balanced, it will have enough representation from all four suits, which tells you that your life is in harmony and that there is balance in your spiritual, material, emotional, and intellectual life. It suggests that you are very flexible when it comes to the way you approach your life. However, in the previously mentioned situation where only one suit predominates your reading, it indicates that you have not been paying attention to other equally important aspects of your life. For instance, in the previous example, you may have been sacrificing your health, love life, and other things on the altar of your financial aspirations.

Reversals

Sometimes when you're reading, you will encounter reversed cards. These cards are not to be ignored because they are extremely powerful, showing you parts of your psyche that may have been hidden or the aspects of your life that you have neglected. These cards show up as a disruption of energy flow. They are reversed because they draw your attention, acting as a clarion call to finally face the obstacles and challenges you have refused to because sticking your head in the sand felt more comfortable. Reverse cards require you to be *comfortable with being uncomfortable.* That's what it'll take to overcome your obstacles and grow and learn from them.

Reversals bring in contrasting energies. These energies are meant to make the reading even more accurate. When cards are upright, this tells you that the energy is free-flowing and that you continue to move forward, building momentum as you do in whatever endeavor you're concerned with. However, a reversed card appears as a challenge to stand against the status quo. Think of it as the representation of delays, the setbacks you deal with, and the conflicts you face on the inside, which no one else knows about. Therefore, you need to look closely at reversed cards when they appear because they have a lot of wisdom you can act on to take your life where you need to go.

Reversed cards will show you the obstacles you've been contending with, even if you have not been willing to look at them because you've been afraid. It is important that when everything is against you, you choose to be unrelenting in your pursuits. You must remain resilient to discover strength you did not know you possessed. This is the gift that reversed cards offer you in a reading.

Another great thing about these cards is that they can demonstrate your life's subconscious, hidden parts. Everyone has a shadow. It doesn't matter what you do to maintain a sunny disposition or how hard you work to always appear nice. Everyone has an aspect of himself that he would prefer to remain hidden in the dark. However, reversed cards force you to plumb the depths of your unconscious mind and finally face your demons. When your demons have been revealed, the good news is you will become much more aware of who you are and what you're capable of, and you will be able to transmute the darkness to light.

The reversed card forces you to come face to face with the truth. In other words, it acts as an obliterator of illusions. It will destroy the lies you have been telling yourself for the longest time. It will also expose other people's true intentions towards you, depending on whether that is the focus of your reading.

Interpreting Reversed Cards

Here are some tips for interpreting reversed cards in the context of other cards:

1. Pay attention to opposing energies in the form of upright counterparts to the reversed cards. For instance, say you noticed an upright King of Diamonds and the reversed Ace of Hearts next to each other. This could demonstrate that you are finding many conflicts between your financial pursuits and your emotional satisfaction.

2. Consider the delays and obstacles you face and whatever area of life you ask the cards about. You must consider the cards surrounding the reversed card because those cards indicate aspects of your life that will be affected by the reversed card's energies. For instance, pulling a 7 of Hearts and a reversed 5 of Spades strongly indicates that you must deal with many more setbacks to achieve your goals.

3. Pay attention to any lingering issues that are yet to be resolved. Sometimes reversed cards are about unfinished business. To determine if this is the case, consider the patterns between reversed cards and the others in the spread. Say you have a reversed 10 of Clubs and the reversed Queen of Diamonds. This could suggest that you're struggling in your career and finances and must pay attention to them, or things will worsen.

4. You should also consider that the reversed cards represent energies hidden within you. They point to the various fears, hidden emotions, and aspects of yourself which you have refused to acknowledge are real. To understand the hidden interplay of the various energies within you, you must look at the cards surrounding the reversed card. An upright Ace of Clubs next to a reversed 9 of Hearts may mean you have continued suppressing your emotional needs or must look at everything about your creativity and passion.

When a Reversed Card Negates an Upright One

It is important to identify when a reversed card simply provides more context versus when it negates outright what an upright card implies. You can figure this out by noticing each card's visual direction in your spread. A card between an upright card and a reversed card shows that while the middle card is affected by the upright card to a degree, the reversed card resists that influence. For instance, assume you have a Queen of Hearts between a King of Hearts and a reversed 8 of Clubs. The King of Hearts is a warm card representing a generous person or someone in touch with their emotions, complementing the Queen of Hearts, which indicates success and influence. On the other hand, the reversed 8 of Clubs shows you that there are challenges regarding your ambitions or your material resources and the possible success coming your way. In this situation, the reversed 8 of Clubs opposes the King of Hearts' influence on the Queen of Hearts.

You must pay attention to the contrast in the symbolism between the reversed card and any upright card that appears energetically or visually connected. When the reversed card has qualities directly the opposite of the upright card, this is a clear sign of negation of the upright card.

Regardless of your preferred method of divining with the cards, you must understand that intuition is key. You cannot rely on your intellect, laws, or memory of each card's meaning. You must tap into the strong voice of your intuition to be properly guided through the otherwise confusing maze of card combinations. To develop this intuition, you must accept and trust what it gives you. The more you trust it, the clearer you'll perceive it, and the more accurate your readings will be in time. It also means spending a significant amount of time with the cards so that you can understand the language they speak to you and sense their energies.

Sample Combinations

Here are a few card combinations and potential interpretations you may draw from them:

Ace of Spades and Seven of Hearts: This could imply the start of something that profoundly changes you or your circumstances (the Ace of Spades) in a way that involves disappointment, or you need to retreat within to gain insight (Seven of Hearts).

Ten of Diamonds and Queen of Clubs: You will experience abundance in your finances (Ten of Diamonds) by being confident, making you charming in your ways (Queen of Clubs), and naturally drawing those people and situations you need to perpetuate said success.

King of Hearts, Ace of Diamonds, and Two of Spades: This refers to someone who is deeply compassionate and giving (King of Hearts) who is likely to bring you great opportunities for success (Ace of Diamonds), even though at the beginning of your connection there will be challenges to overcome (Two of Spades).

Jack of Clubs, Eight of Hearts, and Three of Diamonds: Drawing this combo suggests that there is a youthful person full of ambition (Jack of Clubs) who will find joy (Eight of Hearts) by finally attaining stability in her finances through practical choices (Three of Diamonds).

Five of Spades, Nine of Clubs, Queen of Diamonds, and King of Spades: You will experience a time of change (Five of Spades), and by the time you're on the other side, you will have come into leadership and success, having finished your project or task (Nine of Clubs), and done your best to be wise about your investments (Queen of Diamonds). However, you must be careful not to use your newfound success to cause others heartache or unnecessary trouble (King of Spades).

So, you now know how to understand what a combination of drawn cards tells you and how you can draw meaning from them. How do you actually perform a reading? The next chapter will explain the process.

Chapter Six: Performing a Reading

Cartomancy readings should be approached with the right attitude and adequate preparation. This chapter will show you everything you need to do to give the best reading you can with zero sweat.

Creating Your Sacred Space

The first thing you must do before a cartomancy reading is to create a sacred space. Sacred spaces are important because, for one thing, they will help you with your focus. This craft requires concentration; you cannot afford to be distracted or struggle to get messages in a place full of conflicting energies that may distort the meanings you glean from the cards. When you create a sacred space, you dedicate an area to your practice that allows you to focus on your intuition and be present in the moment.

Sacred spaces are also important because you will conduct rituals and work with powerful imagery. This fact implies that your psychological state will shift in a way that makes it more conducive to receiving messages from intuition and spirits. Sacred spaces help you root your intentions firmly in your mind and create an atmosphere of divinity.

Creating a sacred space also entails preparing energetically and emotionally for your reading. It means you can let go of all distractions and worries, making receiving messages from the cards easier. The sacred space also acts as an energetic and physical boundary that keeps the profane from the profound. This is how to create your sacred space:

Performing your readings in a sacred space can help you work with powerful imagery.

First, choose somewhere quiet and comfortable. Remember, you want *zero distractions*. The space could be in your home or in a nice spot outside.

Next, clear the space. If there's any form of clutter, you should get rid of it because it will likely add to your distractions. Removing the clutter encourages peace of mind and a sense of calmness, making connecting with the cards easier.

Set up the lighting. Lighting is important when you are creating your sacred space. Soft lamps or candles can create a gentle and welcoming atmosphere. Usually, it's best to go with natural light or something warm that allows you to really relax.

Use incense. You can make use of different aromas to affect your mood for the better. Therefore, invest in scented candles, incense sticks, or essential oils for your ritual space. Choose scents that make you feel present and relaxed, making it easier to connect your intuition.

Incorporate music. Music can also affect your mood and set you in a more receptive, open space in your mind. So, consider playing some ambient music that will make the atmosphere feel even more sacred than it does. You could also opt for nature sounds or work with meditation tracks that will allow you to relax.

Now it's time to create your altar. This is an optional step. However, you can create an altar if you feel you must. You can put meaningful images, symbols, crystals, and the cards you will work with on this altar. The altar aims to act as an anchor point where all your attention will be channeled during your readings.

Practicing Meditation

If you want to practice cartomancy, making meditation a daily habit is beneficial. Meditation will help you quiet your mind – which is essential for getting in touch with your intuition. There is no way you can experience the sense of calm needed for an accurate reading if your mind is constantly bothered by stressful thoughts, whether chatter or some distraction, making it tough to connect with your inner wisdom. By meditating, you put yourself in the right state of mind and receive messages from the cards and spirit.

Another important thing is that meditation helps you with your concentration. By meditating regularly, you can maintain your focus on basically any task for as long as you need. This skill is essential when it comes to cartomancy. Because the more concentrated you are on the task, the easier it'll be for you to glean the various meanings, symbolisms, and subtle nuances from the cards as you read.

Meditation is also a powerful way to develop your intuition. When you habitually turn within, you'll find a sure voice that lets you know what you need to know at every point. Everyone has intuition, but not everyone develops it. Consider meditating every day to have the level of connection necessary with your intuition to serve your readings.

Not only does meditation help you think clearly, it will also assist you with sensing energies. As you already know, every card has energy, and you'll be better at sensing it when you have the necessary tools. Meditation will give you heightened awareness, making picking up on subtle energies easy. You'll get such nuanced readings that anyone else working only with the meanings on the card couldn't possibly dream of. You can use two basic meditation methods to improve your cartomancy.

Mindfulness: With this meditation method, you only have to observe the thoughts, feelings, and sensations that you experience without offering any judgment. This is an excellent way to ensure you are always present during your readings. To practice mindfulness, sit in a comfortable position and ensure that you wear comfortable clothing. Ideally, you should be in a space that is free from distractions. If you live with other people, tell them not to bother you for the next 10 to 15 minutes. Sit, shut your eyes, part your lips slightly, inhale through your nose, and then exhale through your lips. As you breathe, pay attention to the breath. Notice how you feel when you inhale and exhale. You may notice that the exhale is longer than the inhale. This is fine. You'll also discover that your mind wanders away from the breath. This is not something to be upset about. In fact, you should be excited about noticing that your mind has wandered. When this happens, gently and lovingly acknowledge that you have been distracted and return your attention to your breath. Do this as often as you need to. The more you do this, the better you'll get at being mindful. Make this a daily practice, and you will see phenomenal results.

Visualization: This method of meditation involves using your imagination to create pictures in your mind. With this methodology, you will find it easier to connect with the pictures on the cards and their colors and what they symbolize on a much deeper level. To practice visualization, once more, find somewhere that is quiet and distraction-free. Shut your eyes, part your lips, inhale through your nose, and exhale through your mouth. Continue to do this until you feel your body relaxing and your mind getting stiller.

Next, picture yourself somewhere peaceful and calm; this could be a beach, a garden, or a mountaintop – whatever works for you is fine. Now, imagine that you're looking at a card. See the card in detail, taking note of all its symbols, colors, and the tiny little details that make that card unique from the others. Get so deep into your visualization that you begin to sense the energies of the cards as you watch them. By doing this every day, you become even better at connecting with the cards and a visual level and gleaning more accurate information from them.

You must remember that you cannot do meditation once and expect the effects to last forever. That would be akin to taking a shower once and assuming you will smell like roses for the rest of your life; meditation is not a fad but a way of life. And it is essential if you are going to practice cartomancy successfully.

Setting Intentions

Setting intentions is important when preparing for reading because this is how you clarify your purpose. This is how you focus your energy to ensure the reading stays on track. To set an intention properly, first, you must figure out why you're conducting a reading to begin with.

Take a moment to think about it. Is there a certain circumstance that you want more clarity on? Are you looking for validation? Do you just want more information on a certain person or aspect of your life? By grasping the motivation for seeking a reading, you will develop a strong intention, and you will guide the cards to give you more accurate answers.

When you figure out why you want to read, the next step is clarifying your intentions and goals. You need to ask yourself what it is you want from the cards. For instance, you may want very specific answers or prefer broad strokes. You may seek to be empowered or to understand something better.

The next step is crafting your intention. Be specific about it. Some people make the mistake of setting general intentions like, "I'd like to know about my financial life." However, it would be more effective to say, "I seek guidance in my present financial situation to understand my strengths and weaknesses and find the opportunities to elevate my finances." When you get very specific with your intention, it makes the reading more focused.

A crucial part of setting intentions is to ensure that you remain receptive. You need to be open to whatever messages you receive. Sometimes, readers will receive messages that they don't agree with, but that doesn't mean the messages aren't true. The last thing you want to do is doubt the cards. When you habitually do this, you're essentially shutting down your intuition and creating a state where your readings are always riddled with uncertainty and, therefore, never accurate. You must stay open and avoid letting your preconceived notions cloud what the card shares with you.

Cleansing and Charging the Deck

Now you have a sacred space and a clear intention. The next step is to cleanse and charge your deck. You cannot skip this step because it is important to eliminate stale, negative energies accumulated on the card and imbue the cards with positive energy that will be good for the reading. You can use the following methods to cleanse your deck.

1. Smudging is a powerful, popular method for cleansing places, people, and things. To "smudge" means to pass the thing you want to cleanse through some smoke. The smoke is often from cleansing herbs like Palo Santo, white sage, or cedar. You will need an incense burner so that you do not hurt yourself. When you light the herbs, you can pass the deck through the smoke. As you do this, envision the smoke removing all negative energies attached to the cards.

2. Another method for cleansing the deck is using salt. Salt cleansing is putting your deck into a container with a little salt and letting it sit overnight. Esoterically, salt is an excellent substance for getting rid of negative or still energies. The next day, brush off all the salt from your cards.

3. You can also give your cards a moonlight bath. This is a great way for you to not only cleanse but charge your deck. All you have to do is set it under the full moon's light. Ensure that it is safe where the elements will not get to your cards and ruin them. You should let them sit in the moonlight overnight so that they can absorb the energies from the moon.

4. Finally, you can try visualization. All you have to do is hold the cards in both hands and then, in your mind, imagine a bright golden light emanating from your hands, surrounding the cards, burning away all negative and stale energies, and charging the cards.

Now that your cards have been cleansed, here are some charging techniques.

1. You can charge your cards with sunlight. It's the same as with moonlight. All you have to do is set your deck of cards somewhere the Sun's light can touch it for hours. It would be best if you worked with the early morning or late afternoon Sun, as the last thing you want is for the Sun to cause the pictures and colors on your card to fade. In your mind, assume the Sun sends energy that charges your cards with love and positivity.

2. You may also work with crystals. All crystals have energy. You can use these energies to charge the deck. You can fig-

ure out which crystal you want to charge your deck with some research. For instance, if you want to specialize in love and romance, you can work with the rose quartz crystal. If you are unsure which crystal to choose for your readings, you may work with clear quartz, which acts as an energy amplifier and goes well with every intention. You may also use amethyst because that stone is known to enhance psychic and intuitive abilities necessary for cartomancy. All you have to do is set the stone on top of your deck for hours or leave it overnight. The cards will take on the positive energy of the crystals. You must make a habit of charging and cleansing your crystals, too.

3. Yet another method to charge your deck involves intentional breathing. All you have to do is hold the deck up to your face and breathe in. As you exhale, imagine that that breath has your intention, and positive energy flows from it and into the cards.

4. You could also work with affirmations. All you have to do is hold the cards in your hands and state positive affirmations like, "I now charge you with love, wisdom, and truth."

Choosing a Spread or Layout

Another important part of preparing for your reading is figuring out the spread or layout you want to work with. To do this, you must think about the purpose of your reading. If you want guidance and something specific or are looking for broad strokes, you will find that those things will affect the spread you choose.

Next, you must consider the complexity and size of your spread. For instance, if you're looking for a simple, generalized answer, you may opt for a one-card draw. However, if you want something more nuanced in detail, you may choose something with multiple cards. If you don't have a lot of time, you may want a spread that doesn't have too many cards involved. If you've got time and you're looking for much deeper insight, it would be best to go with the largest possible layouts.

Formulating Questions

To ask clear questions, take time to reflect on what it is you're going through right now. What is it about? Gather all your feelings and thoughts about the circumstance first. Next, consider the main issue with the circumstance for which you need clarity. When you're clear about what the main objective of your reading is, it's time to craft your question. Make sure that they are specific. It does not help to ask broad questions like "What could the future hold?" Instead, you need to be very specific. For instance, ask, "What can I do to ensure that my relationship continues to improve?"

Note that you will get specific guidance when you are specific with your question. So don't be afraid to get very precise. If time is important regarding the situation, you must incorporate that element into your question. For instance, ask whether you should attend a seemingly important event at a certain time. It is important to specify when the time is, too. Is it within the next two months or in 3 years? Work that into your question.

Go with open-ended questions. These questions will allow the cards to answer you with lots of insight. Asking simple yes or no questions isn't the way to go in cartomancy. You want to ask questions that will cause you to reflect deeply.

Once you finally have your question, reflecting on it and refining it is important. Consider whether it captures everything you seek to understand about your situation and whether it agrees with your intentions for the reading. If you discover you must make adjustments, then do so. When you finally have it clear in your mind, write the question down so that your intention for the reading is fixed in your mind.

Developing Personal Interpretations

Getting better at cartomancy means practicing working with your intuition and fine-tuning that skill. Here are some things you can do to interpret the cards like a pro. First, you should study the cards and get familiar with them. After all, you cannot try to explain what you haven't taken the time to understand. So, think about the imagery, the colors, the various archetypes connected to the card, and so on. This book has provided ample information about the cards you could begin with.

Next, it is important that you just trust your intuition. Whenever a voice speaks up, trust it. It could be an actual voice or just a sense of knowing. It could be a thought with a distinctly different quality than your usual mental chatter. When you feel energy, don't question it or second guess it. Accept that this energy is the truth. With time, you'll discover that you are a lot more confident and your intuition.

Journaling is a good practice to have after each reading. You should write down everything you understood from the reading, the impressions you got from each card, and so on. These notes that you're making should always be reviewed. When you do this, you strengthen your ability to understand each card and interpret them accurately, depending on the context.

Another useful thing to help you with personal interpretations of these cards is to use active imagination exercises so that you can connect with them deeply. The visualization meditation you were offered is a great tool for this.

Consider your personal connection and meanings when it comes to the various images, colors, and symbols on the card. For instance, a card may remind you of a person or event. Do not discount your personal meanings just because they do not align with the traditional interpretations of the card. There may be a way to marry those meanings so that you can understand exactly what is being communicated to you by the divine.

Consider working with other cartomancers in your field. Because when you share your experiences with them, and they share theirs with you, you may pick up a thing or two. It is always a good idea to be open to new ways of doing things. Therefore, connecting with others is good, and staying open and curious will do wonders for your practice. A final note is that you must work with the cards regularly. You can't expect to work with them occasionally and somehow develop proficiency. Do a daily practice, and you will see phenomenal results over time.

Now that you know what you must do to perform a reading, it's time to look at some sample readings to try your hand at the real thing. Head on to the next chapter for this.

Chapter Seven: Sample Readings

Sample readings are essential because they help you practice and use your skills appropriately. This chapter's main goal is to offer practical examples of how cartomancy can be applied in real life.

Sample Three-Card Spread Reading

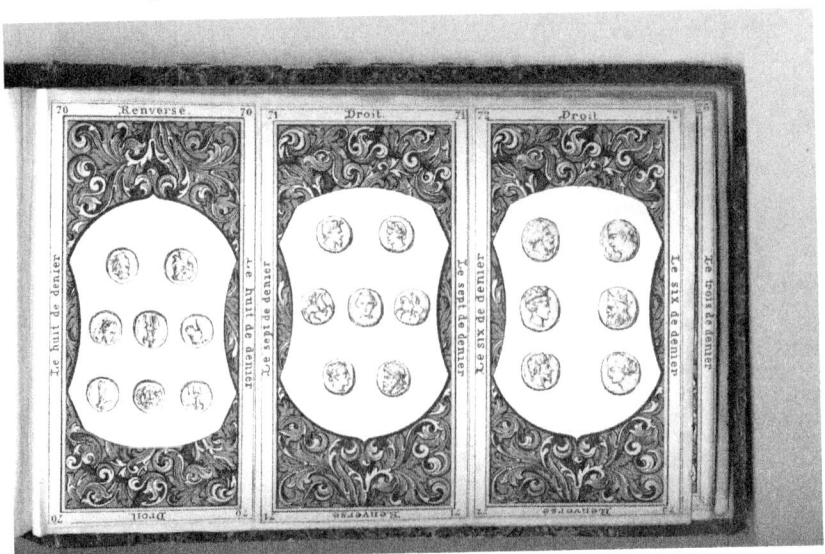

Sample three-card spread.
https://commons.wikimedia.org/wiki/File:Print,_playing-card_(BM_1982,U.4598.1-78_09).jpg

Question: I suspect my partner is cheating on me as she claims to be faithful but posts certain things on social media that would imply to others that she's not in a relationship. Do I have anything to worry about regarding our relationship?

Cards drawn: Ace of Hearts, 5 of Spades, Queen of Diamonds

Card 1: Ace of Hearts

This card represents a new start. It's all about finally feeling fulfilled emotionally and finding the love you have long sought. In the context of the question, this card implies that your relationship is set on a firm foundation rooted in love and true connection. The connection between you and your partner is genuine, and you both feel deep affection for one another. It states that the bond cannot easily be broken and that if you both allow it, there is a potential for you to create something beautiful that lasts a lifetime. Look at everything going on with your relationship and cherish it. It's asking you to do what you can to foster this relationship so that it continues to improve.

Cards 2: 5 of Spades

This card represents conflict, obstacles, and challenges. It suggests you and your partner may butt heads now and then, experiencing difficult situations and having disagreements. However, you must not be quick to make assumptions or jump to conclusions. The 5 of Spades tells you that forces outside your relationship or misunderstandings could create tension. You may be misinterpreting this tension as possible infidelity. Therefore, you must do your best to stay open. Communicate your feelings with your partner to address any issues that may crop up in that conversation. By choosing to communicate, you create a situation where your challenges can easily be overcome, and not only that, your relationship can be stronger and better for it.

Card 3: Queen of Diamonds

This card embodies the energies of loyalty, stability, and practicality. Considering your question, this card tells you your partner is the bastion of stability and loyalty. The Queen of Diamonds stays faithful no matter what and always has the bigger picture in her mind. This person understands the importance of her connections and intends to stay committed to you. This card implies that your partner wants nothing but to ensure you both have a strong, long-lasting foundation. Therefore, this card asks you to trust that your partner is truly faithful to you and appreciate that.

Sample Celtic Cross Reading

Question: My sister and her husband threw me out of their home when I was in a vulnerable position with my mental health, and they never reached out to me once in 8 years. Finally, they have and claim they want to make amends and help me financially. Still, I suspect they're only planning to use me in a scheme against a step-sibling I'm close to (the person they've taken to court over frivolous claims). How should I approach their offer to help?

Card 1 — The Present: 3 of Hearts

This card suggests healing and a chance to reconcile with your family. It implies that the situation may offer a chance to fix the hurts from the past and mend broken bridges. It tells you that you have a shot here to forgive and be forgiven and understand each other.

Card 2 — Current Challenge: 10 of Diamonds

In this context, the ten of diamonds implies that what you are facing right now is whether or not your sister and her husband's offer to assist you is sincere. This card asks you to be careful in considering their intentions for you.

Card 3 — Distant Past: King of Clubs

The energy of the King of Clubs is someone who has authority and a strong will. In the past, there were power dynamics that did not favor you in your relationship with your family. The constant conflict led to misunderstandings. Perhaps you were labeled the black sheep. This card asks you to consider the dynamics between yourself and this person (your sister and her husband in this situation). Think about how their actions have affected your current situation and how likely it is that they may have changed.

Card 4 — Recent Past: 8 of spades

The 8 of Spades is a card that represents challenges on your path. Not too long ago, you had to deal with limitations and difficulties that stressed you mentally. These situations may have been further aggravated by the fact that you were thrown out of your home. Therefore, this card indicates that you were struggling terribly at that time and probably still are.

Card 5 — Best Outcome: Queen of Hearts

This card represents the energy of nurturing and compassion. It is all about being supported emotionally. If you accept your sister and her husband's proposal, do so cautiously while keeping your heart open, as there is a chance that you can be truly reconciled to each other.

Card 6 — Future Influence: 7 of Diamonds

The 7 of Diamonds tells you that there is a chance for you to grow financially. So, when it comes to the assistance being offered, there is a possibility that your financial situation could be better. However, it would be wise for you to be discerning. In other words, if you accept their help, it is important not to put yourself in a position where you will remain indebted to them. In fact, it may be best to tell them that you accept their offer and are thankful for it, but that does not automatically mean that they gain access to you or the right to control you as they did in the past.

Card 7 — Inner Emotions: Ace of Spades

This card represents new beginnings and fresh changes. Regarding your internal emotions, the card clarifies that you are very skeptical about their intentions. You really want to believe they have only the best intentions for you, but you can't help but be uncertain. You want a fresh start with them, but you are clearly troubled that this may be more of the same old dynamics you've already experienced with them. You need to trust your instincts and listen to your intuition to discern if or when you must remove yourself from interactions where they are concerned.

Card 8 — External Influences: 2 of Spades

This card represents challenges and obstacles. So, in this case, the challenge is the court case that involves your step-sibling. There is a great possibility that your sister and her husband are reaching out to you only because they feel like you would be a critical part of them winning the case they have with your step-sibling. It is up to you to decide if you want to accept their help while being clear if the time comes that you are not willing to be blackmailed into doing the wrong thing.

Card 9 — Hopes and Fears: Jack of Diamonds

This card is about being practical and resourceful in your ways. It demonstrates that you have hope that this could be the thing that finally plants you solidly on your feet financially. However, you are afraid that you will only be taken advantage of or become entangled in something that betrays your step-sibling.

Card 10 — Final Outcome: 4 of Clubs

This card tells you that your choices must be structured and ordered. In other words, you must be practical about this situation. There is a chance that you could finally be uplifted financially, as it sounds like you have been struggling with that. Just because you were suspicious of their intentions does not mean you should completely shove them aside, as they may be willing to offer you the help you need. You must, however, remain in touch with your instincts so that if it becomes obvious that they are attempting to weasel their way back into your life to control you, you can promptly cut ties. In the meantime, ask questions, and be honest with them and yourself.

Sample Three-Card Spread Reading

Question: Lately, I've felt the need to get more serious with my spiritual life. Still, I don't know where to start – how can I develop a bond with my higher self?

Card 1 — The Past: Queen of Hearts

Since this card represents compassion, you may have had certain experiences that piqued your spiritual curiosity and made you aware that there's much more to life than meets the eye. These experiences served as the seed for your present desire to connect with your spiritual nature. In your past, you experienced things that triggered you to become deeply sensitive to the subtle energies of the spiritual realm. In other words, you already have a good foundation to begin your spiritual exploration.

Card 2 — The Present: 8 of Diamonds

This card represents your discipline and practicality in manifesting the abundance that awaits you. The card implies that to connect with your higher self, finding disciplined and practical methods to help you along your path would be best. In other words, whatever spiritual path you choose should be structured and grounded. This is because these are the paths most likely to be effective at demonstrating to you just how spiritual you are. Therefore, you should study spiritual teachings with verifiable, observable impacts and results.

Card 3 — The Future: Ace of Spades

The Ace of Spades is the card of new spiritual insights and changes. This card tells you that you will experience a profound connection with your higher self in the future. This means that you will spiritually awaken and transform. The wisdom and insight you will receive as you walk your spiritual path will be life-changing. The Ace of Spades also implies that you will experience many opportunities to develop and grow as a spiritual being and connect with your higher self even more strongly than you can imagine.

Question: Lately, I've noticed that my body isn't acting like it used to. I am concerned but don't want to trouble myself needlessly. What must I be aware of to ensure I remain physically whole and youthful?

(Please note that you should always seek medical attention from a licensed professional if you feel there's something wrong with your body. Cartomancy is only a tool to give you further insight, not to diagnose you.)

Card 1 – The Present: Joker

The Joker is a card of unpredictability. It implies being flexible and having a sense of humor. Now, in the context of the question asked, the Joker represents the current situation that your body is going through. There are changes in its usual function that have you concerned. The Joker asks you to consider these changes with a flexible and open mindset. You are being asked to embrace the change and find a balance between caring for yourself and letting yourself enjoy life. The Joker tells you that not everything should be taken seriously and that it would be best to maintain a sense of humor about your health, as this will do wonders for it in the long run.

Card 2 – The Challenge: Queen of Hearts

The Queen of Hearts represents your emotional well-being. This card is about your intuition and your ability to nurture yourself. Related to your question, the card tells you that the challenge is trying to understand your emotions, which may have a powerful impact on your physical health. What you think is a physical problem is actually rooted in your emotions. The card tells you that you must pay attention to your feelings and do what you can to bring yourself more joy, laughter, and fulfillment. It is a good idea to ensure you have supportive relationships full of love and positivity. When you take care of your emotional well-being, it reflects on your body positively.

Card 3 – Guidance and Outcome: 7 of Diamonds

This card represents the ideas of being resourceful and practical. It is also about financial matters. Relative to your question, the card implies that it would be best to notice what you need physically. For instance, your body may ask you for more rest, exercise, or better nutrition. Therefore, you need to be practical in solving your current physical challenges. This card tells you that you should also consider investing money into maintaining your health and making decisions that will ultimately benefit you.

In summary, this reading asks you to be at peace with the changes that your body experiences, invest in taking care of yourself, and take the time to make sure you feel good emotionally. Put money into yourself and your health because you deserve it. Try to find balance in every part of your life, and you will find that your concerns are not much to worry about.

Now that you've seen a few readings, it is time for you to take your craft to the next level by working with your intuition. You're going to discover how in the next chapter. But first, let's talk about intuition. What is it?

Chapter Eight: Intuitive Readings

What Is Intuition?

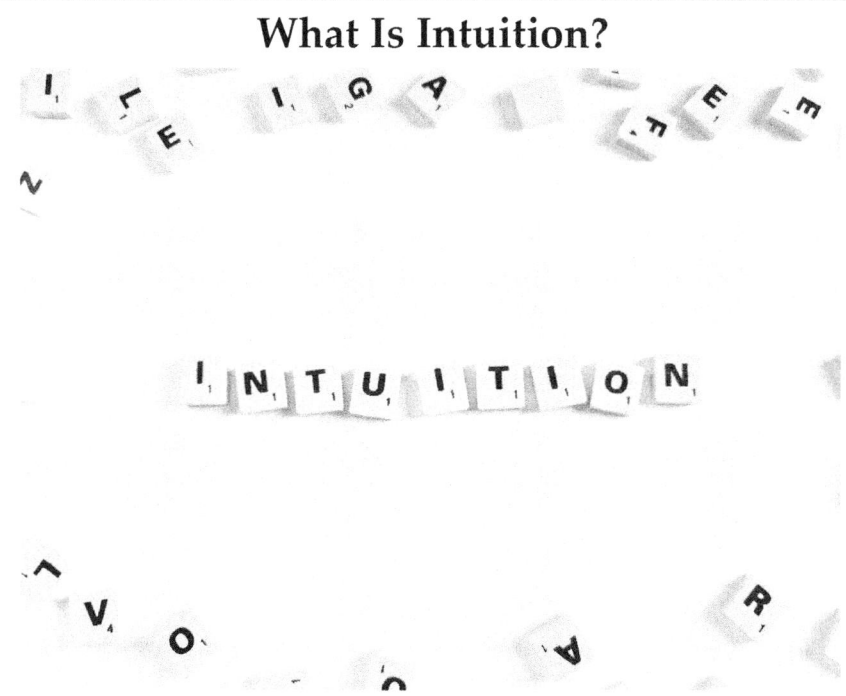

Intuition is a force beyond logic and reason.
https://unsplash.com/photos/j5itvdU55FI

Intuition has been mentioned several times in this book. But the question is, what is it, truly? Intuition is something that exists in everyone. You can think of it as an ancient mystical force responsible for the evolution of consciousness as it is today. Intuition is something that is beyond the bounds of logic and reason. It comes from your soul, that voice that tells you things that are spot on. Intuition is when you get sudden knowledge about something in a way that you cannot quite describe. You just know it's true, and when you check on your hunch, you discover you were right about it. Your intuition is that aspect of you that uncovers all the secrets of the universe and lets you know what's happening beneath the surface of every situation.

It is important to realize that intuition is not just a fleeting thought. It is not something that you deduce by logical thinking. It is much more than that. Most logically-inclined people tend to assume that intuition is the same thing as a deduction, but it is not. Intuition involves emotions and a deep inner knowing that comes from beyond your mind. It ripples through the essence of your soul and being. Intuition can communicate to you through various means, such as synchronicity, signs, and symbols all around you.

Interestingly, intuition also surpasses the bounds of time and space. It doesn't matter whether you're dealing with your past, present, or future. Intuition can make itself available, revealing everything you need to know about any time in your life or any experience you might have had.

When performing cartomancy, you must be in touch with this inner wisdom you carry. Unfortunately, many people have dulled this sense because they continue to indulge in habits that do not serve their intuition. For instance, if you spend a lot of time on social media or indulge in certain substances that affect or alter your consciousness, you may find your intuitive edge dull. However, there's nothing to worry about because you can always sharpen it when you want to. And you will learn just how to do that to have the most intuitive, bang-on readings during your cartomancy sessions.

How Intuition Works

Attuning yourself to sense subtle energies: To conduct intuitive readings, it is important for you to first understand the mechanics of intuition. The first thing involves sensing what is unseen or undetectable to your five senses. When you can connect to the unseen, you've opened yourself up to the secrets in the spiritual realm. If you don't already know this, know that everything physical is rooted in the spiritual world. In other words, the spiritual energy permeates everything and everyone that exists. Consequently, by developing your intuition, you set up a situation where you are more open to picking up the subtle energies of spirit, which implies that you can access any information you want regardless of space or time. This is because the spiritual aspect of life transcends those two boundaries of space and time.

Paying attention to your inner wisdom: The next step in connecting to your intuition involves listening to your inner wisdom. Once you can attune yourself to subtle energies by using practices like meditation, you must teach yourself to listen to the inner voice that speaks within you. Everyone has this voice, but the more you practice paying attention to it, and the better you are at picking up subtle energies, the louder is voice will be. It'll be tough to mistake it for anything else.

Some people assume that these voices are a result of mental conditions like schizophrenia, or they feel that these voices are pretty much the same as a thought that you have in your head, but that's not the case at all. Something about intuition speaking usually freezes you in your tracks and causes you to take stock of the present moment as all time and space lose meaning. You know deep within yourself that the information you're getting is accurate. Listening to the wisdom within you means you must tune out the world's noise outside and focus all your attention on the inside.

Trusting strange things: The next thing you must do after tuning yourself to subtle energies and learning to listen to your inner voice is to trust what feels unfamiliar. This is important because intuitive messages will often show up in ways that are not the norm for you. After all, how else are they supposed to get your attention? Intuition can be a gut feeling, knowing, a hunch that you're right about something, or even a flash of insight. To get better at working with your intuition and having it be more accurate, you must learn to trust it in whatever form it shows up for you. Do not fall into the trap of questioning whether or not what it shares with you is true. Intuition is one of those things where *when you know, you know.*

Paying attention to symbols and synchronicity: Recognizing synchronicity and symbolism is a huge part of understanding your intuition and working with it. Symbols are the language of the subconscious. Synchronicity is how your soul attempts to communicate with you through your intuition. Synchronicity is the unlikeliness of certain events happening simultaneously or in line with one another in a way that cannot be logically explained. It involves seeing a certain number pattern repeating itself or having a set of events play out so beautifully that you could not have imagined it. You need to learn to recognize synchronicity and other symbols that can pop up in your daily life. The more attention you pay to these things and listen to your intuition, the more you can learn about life.

Working on being in the present: Developing mindfulness is the next thing you must consider. In other words, you must teach yourself to be in the here and now. Often, most people are stuck ruminating about their past or worrying about their future but never really pay attention to what's happening here and now. For you to connect with your intuition, you must be present. This is because intuition thrives in the here and now. So, if you're hoping to get guidance from this inner wisdom you carry daily, you must master the art of always staying grounded in the present. And the way to do this is by practicing being mindful. Meditation is one way you can achieve mindfulness.

Accepting the wisdom of your heart: It is funny that many assume that wisdom only comes from the brain. However, this is not always the case. Your heart has a wisdom of its own. That wisdom is intuition. You must learn the language of emotions because this is how your intuition will often speak to you. That's not to say that intuition is only about how you feel. However, you need to know what your heart tells you at every point in time because that is how you get better at working with your intuition. Your intuition is not a logical thing. It is mostly emotional. Therefore, by getting familiar with your emotional landscape, you will find yourself accessing amazing wells of knowledge you could never have fathomed.

With all this said, the question is, how do you perform an intuitive reading? How can you develop and harness your intuition in the practice of cartomancy?

Well, you're about to discover just how!

You already know two excellent methods to get in touch with your intuition and develop it. As discussed in the previous chapter, you can use meditation and visualization exercises. However, the following are ways you can develop your intuition to have more intuitive readings.

Mindful Observation

Mindful observation is exactly the way it sounds. It is all about paying attention to everything happening within and around you. It is about noticing your environment, thoughts, feelings, emotions, and sensations. The more you pay attention to these things, the more present you will feel, which is a bonus for your intuitive readings. Here's how to practice mindful observation:

1. First, you must find somewhere quiet where you will not be distracted or disturbed for at least 10 to 15 minutes. Ensure that this location allows you to relax easily and wear comfortable clothing.

2. Sit in a position that is comfortable for you. If you like, you can sit cross-legged, or you can sit on a chair. Put your hands on your thighs or just rest them in your lap however you want to.

3. Take some time to ground yourself. This means you will shut your eyes and take a few deep breaths in through your nose and out through your mouth. Allow your body to get less tense with each exhale. Notice the weight of your body and allow it to let go of all the tension you feel.

4. Notice your breath. This is basically the same as meditation. Sit with your breath and observe it as it goes in and out.

5. Now, it's time to go beyond this by expanding your awareness. This implies that you will begin to allow other information besides your breath to filter into your mind. Start noticing your thoughts, how you feel, and the emotions you are sensing. Notice them as they come up but do your best not to judge any of them. Don't get attached, as you're just observing.

6. It's time to bring your senses into the game. Notice the smells, sights, and sensations you're picking up with your five senses. You must engage with every sensory impression as fully as you can.

7. Do your best to remain non-judgmental. Continue to observe all these things and let go of the need to attach a label to any of them. Just observe curiously and with acceptance.

8. When your mind inevitably wanders from the exercise, as it will, just gently bring it back to the present. Get back to focusing on your breath and your observations. It is all about being aware, so keep that in mind.

9. Finally, you must practice this as often as you can. This is how you get better at being mindfully observant.

Now, you're probably wondering the difference between this exercise and the meditation exercise you were given before. Remember that where the meditation exercise has you only focusing on your breath, this mindful observation exercise is about you becoming aware of other things besides your breath that will help you be rooted in the present moment.

Intuitive Exercises

Intuitive exercises are wonderful tools for helping you get better at using your intuition during cartomancy. Here's how you can get involved with them.

1. Pick an exercise. For instance, you may choose an exercise like trying to guess what's in a sealed envelope or intuitively picking cards from a deck, guessing what's on the card, before flipping it around to see if you were correct.

2. Now that you know the exercise you want, set your intention. Your intention involves getting better at working with your intuition and getting accurate information. You can state the sensation out loud or in your mind.

3. Make sure you're somewhere where the weather is no disturbance or distraction. If it helps, you can set up the ambiance with perfect lighting, music, and even incense.

4. It's time to relax and calm yourself with a few breaths. When you feel like your mind is clear and your body is relaxed, you can move on to the next step.

5. Begin guessing what's in your sealed envelopes. Let your intuition be your guide, and don't try to rush the process. It is important to note that there is no force in the process regarding your intuition. So be as relaxed and at ease as you can be. If you notice that you're picking the wrong things or making the wrong guesses, it is important not to be hard on yourself because that may only cause you to have even worse results.

6. When you've finished your exercise, reflect on your results. Compare how accurate your guesses were this time as opposed to the last time. And also, it is important to ensure that

you practice regularly.

Other Tools to Sharpen Intuition

In addition to the tools offered so far, there are other things you can do to sharpen your intuitive senses. Here is a quick look at them:

1. **Keep a journal.** When you keep a journal, you start to take stock of your life. It means that you become more aware of how you are changing and how your world is changing. Becoming aware naturally means you will become more sensitive to your intuitive voice. Consider writing down your dreams and every intuitive hunch you get. Also, when you notice something synchronistic going on, write it down. For instance, if you notice that you keep seeing a certain number all the time, it might be worth noting what's happening around you and the thoughts and feelings you were having when the number showed up. You may notice that there is a pattern there. Always review your journal. It's not just about writing things down but reading them later to help you start spotting intuition at work in your life.

2. **Try energy work.** You naturally become more sensitive to subtle energies when you do energy work such as Reiki or Qigong. As you already know, intuition can speak to you through subtle energies in addition to your emotions. Therefore, any form of energy work at all but help you to begin picking up on vibes. This goes even beyond cartomancy as you adapt to reading people because you've been practicing how to work with energy.

3. **Express yourself creatively.** Something about the creative process does wonders when opening up your intuitive abilities and making them more pronounced. You should do it, whether writing, painting, or making music. The wonderful thing about creative activities is that they're an excellent way for you to bypass your logical, rational mind and gain access to the intuitive side of yourself.

4. **It is a good idea to spend as much time around nature as you can.** The more time you spend in nature, connecting with a natural world that is naturally in alignment with spiritual energies and subtle energies, the better you will understand

when it is your intuition speaking.

5. **Finally, you will find much value in solitude**. This doesn't mean you should never have friends, go out, or communicate with your family. It just means that you must practice finding time to retreat and be on your own each day. This is because you need to distinguish between your intuitive voice and your thoughts, as well as your intuitive voice versus those of other people around you. You need to be separated for a bit every day because that is how you become familiar with the voice of spirit, and this will go a long way and help you with the accuracy of your readings.

Cultivating an Open Mind

Working with your intuition implies having an open and receptive mind. If your mind is closed off and constantly questioning things, then the odds are you will not have much success with your readings. Therefore, there are a few things that you should consider incorporating into your daily practices:

- Make a practice of clearing your mind before you start reading.
- Let go of the desire for a reading to go in a specific way. Every reading is unique and doesn't always have to play out how you think it should.
- Do your best not to judge. Your only job is to channel the message from the cards and nothing more. Playing judge, jury, and executioner during reading is not your job.
- You must develop trust for your inner wisdom. This is the only way you can continue to encourage your intuition to feed you all the information you need and pick up on it accurately.
- You must always be compassionate to yourself. You're just learning, which means you'll make some mistakes. It's not a good idea to beat yourself up just because you get some things wrong while learning to become a cartomancy master. So, give yourself some time and love.
- Take care of yourself physically, mentally, and emotionally, and you will discover that your intuition improves.

Follow all of the tips offered in this chapter. You will discover that you become better each day at working with your intuition in every situation, not just during your cartomancy readings. Now that you understand how to develop the muscle of your intuition, the question is: *is there more to cartomancy?* In the next chapter, you're going to learn some advanced cartomancy.

Chapter Nine: Advanced Carto-mancy

Hold on to your horses because the techniques you will learn in this chapter are not for the newbies. You could attempt them if you are new to cartomancy. Still, it would be much better for you to understand the basics before attempting either method.

The Wheel of Fortune Spread

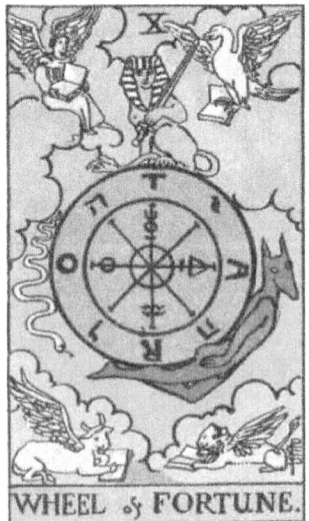

Wheel of Fortune tarot card represents change.

In Tarot, there is a card known as the Wheel of Fortune. This card represents the energy of cycles, chance, changes, and fortune. Its darker aspects include repetition, destiny, fate, and recurrences. There is a spread that is based on this particular card. This spread is founded on the idea of seasons, reminiscent of the idea of cycles represented by the Wheel of Fortune. The thing about cycles is that you cannot escape them. And in the same way, you cannot turn back the hands of time.

As you pay attention to life's seasons, you realize there is a time to act and another to hang back and observe. It is important to detect the harmonies that are naturally inherent in life so that we can flow with them. Most people live their lives trying to force things to happen when they should be resting or hibernating. Humans are not divorced from nature. Therefore, you must follow its rhythm. Otherwise, you will find yourself living a life of misery. This is the wisdom embodied in the Wheel of Fortune card and the concept of the wheel itself.

A good time to use this spread is when you want to look at your life's events from a broad perspective or see how your year has been so far and how your life has changed since the start of a new year.

The Wheel of Fortune spread has six cards. The first card to be dealt is the Self card in the middle and to the left. It represents what your current state is. The second card is the Environment card, which goes to the right of the Self card. This talks about the world you find yourself in and how it influences you and your actions. The third card is the Winter card, the solo card on top of the middle row of four. This card lets you know that it is time to rest or hibernate so that you can regain your strength. It talks about what you need to take a break from at the moment or what you need to renew.

The fourth card is the Spring card, which sits to the extreme left on the fourth row. This card tells you about your growth. It'll show you what is just coming to be in your life or what is building momentum.

The fifth, or summer card, is at the bottom of the entire spread and represents abundance. This is a time in your life when everything blooms fully. So, it calls you to appreciate or be thankful for the good in your life right now.

The sixth card is the fall card, the extreme right on the four-card row. This card represents losing or passing on. It's about what to let go of or what is leaving your life now.

Working with the Wheel of Fortune spread is easy now that you understand how these cards are laid out and their meanings. Remember that all you have to do is apply the concepts from previous chapters about interpreting cards relative to one another.

The Zodiac Tarot Spread

The Zodiac spread is also called the 12-house astrology spread. It is commonly used with a Tarot deck. You can read it in one or two ways, either informatively or predictively. In other words, you can read it by gleaning meaning from the astrological house of each card, or you can use each card to represent a month of the year and predict what your month may be like.

Since the Zodiac spread works with all the astrological houses, of which there are 12, it's a good spread for you to use when you're just looking for a general idea of where your life is going. The 12 astrological houses also represent the 12 different aspects of your life. So, if you want to ask some really pointed questions like what your love life will look like over the next year, this is an excellent spread to work with.

You need to know some things before you begin working with the spread. First, there are many variations of the Zodiac tarot spread, and you'll learn one of the easiest. If you have some knowledge of astrology, it might be worth looking into the other more complicated ways of working with this spread.

Another thing you must remember about the spread is that it's best to do it occasionally. In other words, this is not something that you work with every day to plan your weeks. It would be best to use this to plan out your year, or at least plan for each quarter. It's also an excellent spread to work with when it's your birthday. If you're worried about how you're supposed to remember all 12 of the astrological houses, the good thing is you can always find this information on the internet. You will work with 12 or 13 cards to set up the Zodiac tarot spread. The final decision is up to you. These cards are going to be set up in a circle.

First, shuffle and cut the deck, and then you put the first card at the far left. This card will be in the 9 o'clock position. Next, you will set the remaining cards on the table or counterclockwise, setting one card for every hour of your imaginary clock. If you're working with a 13th card, put that card in the middle of the circle you have created. It is important to know astrology because you must understand that each card represents the various houses and signs of the Zodiac, beginning with Aries.

The first card represents the **Sun sign**. Your Sun sign is the general astrological sign people ask you about when they ask what your sign is. The Sun sign is associated with the First House or the House of Self. It represents your general personality, how you view life and present yourself to the world. It's about how you see yourself and how others perceive you. This House also represents your health.

The second card represents the **House of Value and Possessions**. It demonstrates how you relate to your finances and your material possessions. It's about your sense of security in life and how much you can earn. The second card is about your self-worth too. It shows you the things that you value the most in life.

The third card represents the **House of Communication**. It's all about your family and the other people around you. It's about who knows you and who you know. But it's important to note that it does not include your children, spouse, or parents. This third card is about your travel as well. If you're working with a tarot, getting six swords in this placement may show that you just might be about to move to someplace new. Communication and writing are also under the purview of this third card.

The fourth card represents the fourth House, the **House of Home and Family**. It demonstrates your relationships with the people at home, especially with your children and parents. This card is a representation of all the attachments that you have gathered throughout your life. It's about your true roots and what domestic living is like for you. It's also the about your emotional stability and security, especially regarding familial ties.

The fifth card correlates with the fifth **House of Astrology**, the **House of Creativity**. It's about the things that you are most passionate about and how you express your emotions physically. This card is all about the hobbies you would like to do for fun and how you approach problem-solving. It's also quite informative about the kind of lover that you are to your significant other. With this card correlated to the 5th House, you can learn what you love in others and what makes you fall in love.

The sixth card is about your work and is associated with the **House of Service**. Not only does it demonstrate how healthy you are on the inside, but it also talks about your self-care, personal hygiene, the way you feed yourself, and so on. This card is about what your everyday habits are.

The seventh card represents your partnerships and correlates to the seventh **House of Relationships.** It is about how you treat the partnerships you have in your life, romantically or otherwise. It lets you know the kind of person who would work best with you regardless of your endeavor. Even enemies are partners, so keep that in mind as you read this card.

The eighth card represents your secrets. It's connected to the **House of Transformation**, all about everything nobody wants to discuss, like sex and death. Maybe even taxes. This card is about what others give you, like gifts, inheritances, or winning a prize or the lottery. Consider what this card holds for you whenever you want to make a big financial decision. The eighth House is the container of your life force and sexual power. In this context, sexual power is not about making love, which is the purview of the fifth House, but is more about the main driving force in your life.

The ninth card is connected to the **House of Purpose**, which is all about your personal growth and dreams. It's about how you can continue to stretch and expand your awareness. This includes travel, further education, philosophy, spirituality, and religion.

The tenth card represents your career and the **House of Social Status**. It represents how you appear. It's not about how you deliberately present yourself, as that would be the first House, but how others see you. It's about the way you are going about making your dreams happen and fulfilling the expectations that you have of yourself. This card has to do with your career and your financial position.

The eleventh card is connected to the **House of Friendships**. It is about your casual friendships, social connections, the people who know you, and how you interact with them. It's also all about charity, shedding light on how you feel about generosity, giving, and worthy causes.

The twelfth card represents your shadow self. It is correlated to the **12th House of Astrology, The House of the Subconscious**. Sometimes you may hear it ominously referred to as the **House of Sorrows**, and this is because it is deeply connected to the psychological issues that you have not addressed yet. This House demonstrates the things that weigh you down and keep you up at night and the self-imposed prison you have created around you through your limiting beliefs. It is a card that demonstrates the enemies that hide within that you may not be aware of, as well as dangers that you have not become conscious of yet. It is this card that will show you if you are living up to your life's potential or not.

Finally, there's the thirteenth card. This card demonstrates the overarching theme of the reading that you are conducting. It is an optional card; however, if you're working with it, it'll give you even more clarity on what the other cards are about.

Specialized Systems

There are specialized decks and systems that you can work with to make your cartomancy practice not only advanced but give you the most detailed interpretations and readings ever. You already know about some of these systems, like the Lenormand cards, Kipper cards, and Tarot cards. However, you can incorporate other specialized systems like rune stones, numerology, and astrology. These are just some ways to tweak your cartomancy readings for deeper meaning.

Runestones, for instance, are powerful ancient symbols in Norse divination. The stones are usually made of actual stones or wood. On each one, you'll find a runic symbol etched into it. Each symbol represents different aspects of life and offers guidance in its own way. To interpret runes accurately, you must understand what each means and determine what various combinations would imply. However, runes are outside the scope of this book. But if you were to learn about them, they would be a wonderful addition to your divination practice with cards.

You've already witnessed through the Zodiac spread how it's possible to incorporate astrology into your readings. However, knowing that you need not use only the Zodiac spread for astrological meanings is important. You can always incorporate astrology by assigning various astrological planets or meanings to the cards.

Numerology is also an excellent way to make your cartomancy system even more specialized. This has already been touched on in a previous chapter, where the significance of numbers was also discussed. It would be worthwhile to dive into numerology even further. Not only can you use numerology by working with the numbers already on the cards, but you can also work with the numbers by counting or taking note of the orders in which the cards were set down on the table during your reading.

When you mix and match different systems of cartomancy and divination, you will find that the results from your readings are powerful. This is because you have access to so many more symbols and meanings that it is impossible not to have a richer perspective of the situation you are asking questions about. You could combine different specialized decks or start off with a Tarot spread so you can understand general themes and then segue into a Lenormand deck to get the specifics. There are no hard and fast rules for practicing cartomancy.

The next chapter will explore the many different approaches to cartomancy. By looking at these different approaches, you will have a much more insightful understanding of how card reading works so that you can develop your own system.

Chapter Ten: Different Approaches to Cartomancy

There are so many approaches you can take when it comes to cartomancy. There's no such thing as the one way that you should take. In fact, there are as many approaches as there are cartomancy practitioners. Therefore, you should not feel restricted to taking just one route. In this chapter, you'll learn about the different approaches you can work with to help you read the cards accurately and intuitively for yourself and the people who seek your services.

Many approaches can be taken to understand cartomancy.
Museum Rotterdam, CC BY-SA 3.0 <https://creativecommons.org/licenses/by-sa/3.0>, via Wikimedia Commons:
https://commons.wikimedia.org/wiki/File:Spel_handgeschreven_kaarten_met_spreuken,_objectn r_32256.JPG

The Analytical Approach

When you're reading the cards using the analytical approach, it implies that you're taking really complex readings and breaking them down so that they're simpler and easier to understand. In other words, you're taking the whole and breaking it down into smaller parts, making it easier for you to use reason and logic to interpret what you're getting from the cards. You're doing some critical analysis and working systematically to discover the true meaning the cards are showing you.

The first thing is to analyze the cards one after the other. In other words, rather than figuring out how two cards generate an entirely new meaning outside of what each one represents, you should look at each card individually. You'll consider traditional meanings, what the card means to you personally, and its symbolism. Look at the colors and imagery on the card to figure out the impressions you're getting from it on an energetic level.

Working analytically means that you must also consider the relationships between the cards. So, think about how close they are in terms of positions (the closer the cards are in a spread, the stronger their influence on each other). Consider how they are in terms of orientation. Is there a card that is reversed next to one which is upright? Which card comes first? Think about the various connections, oppositions, or patterns they show up.

You must bring logic and reason into play. This means that you will use deductive reasoning and some critical thinking to determine what the card combinations are trying to tell you. This does not mean you won't use your intuition in this approach. However, you will rely mostly on your logical mind for this process.

You should have a set framework that allows you to easily analyze the cards every single time. You're definitely not going to get away with not paying attention to details when you choose the analytical method of cartomancy. This approach is about being as objective as possible when interpreting the cards.

Predictive Approach

Choosing the predictive route instead of the analytical route implies that you will interpret the cards to figure out what could happen in the future regarding a certain situation. You will also have to work with symbols here because you have to interpret the symbols' meanings relative to possible future results. Each card will have its unique archetype, energy, and situation that you can use to draw conclusions about what you could expect to come.

Another important element of this method of approach is the timing and progression of things. You may want to think about where the positions of the cards are, astrology, numerology, and other methodologies to figure out just when something happens, what will happen, and in what sequence. This makes it easier for you to create a timeline of possible events that may occur.

When working with a predictive approach, consider the probability of something specific happening over something else. In other words, you must consider that there will be alternatives to your possible future predictions. When you allow for some flexibility here, it gives you more room for nuanced predictions. It allows you to be better prepared for whatever scenario comes your way.

When working with a predictive approach, you must be as ethical as possible. In other words, if you're doing a reading for someone else, you must continue to let the querent understand that their results are not necessarily set in stone and can always change. You must support whoever asks questions by helping them understand that they are in charge of their destiny. There is no such thing as something being fixed in stone regarding their cartomancy results.

Therapeutic Approach

You can work with a therapeutic approach when you want to use the readings to help you grow personally or reflect on your life. You can also use this as a healing tool. The cards can help you understand what's going on with your health and well-being emotionally, psychologically, and spiritually. A therapeutic approach to cartomancy aims to help you become more aware of yourself – and can help with empowerment in that area.

This approach to reading the cards involves a lot of introspection and self-reflection. Because the cards act as a mirror that shows you how you've been thinking and feeling both consciously and subconsciously and how all of this has come together to create the life that you have lived so far, another thing to note is that you must explore your emotions when working with this approach. You should think about your emotions and what's causing them. In other words, the cards will act as a shovel to dig beneath the surface and uncover whatever is lying beneath emotionally. This way, you can let go of the blockages holding you back from experiencing clarity and progress in life.

The therapeutic approach also implies that you will use the cards to help you heal whatever wounds you suffer emotionally and spiritually. You can use the cards with this approach to deal with the challenges and obstacles on your path to feel more empowered and take control of your life.

This approach also implies working with symbols and metaphors. You must be in touch with your empathetic and compassionate side because it is important not to be judgmental while making inquiries on your or another person's behalf. With this method, you can set your intentions and goals based on the information you get from the cards. If you choose, you can also integrate this therapeutic approach of cartomancy with other therapies such as psychotherapy, counseling, or energy healing. All of this will augment the results you get from your card reading sessions.

The Narrative Approach

In cartomancy, the narrative approach involves working with stories to understand what the cards say. As a reader, crafting a narrative that offers insights and clear guidance is your job. One of the first things you must do is create the storyline, which means you must look at the cards as if they are trying to tell you a story. You must consider the cards as one, looking for the characters, plot lines, and other elements you typically find in a story.

Another important element of this narrative approach requires considering the sequence of the cards in their placements. This sequencing will offer you more understanding as you craft the story, which must come from intuition. You shouldn't feel like you're forcing the process. As you read the cards in a story format, you can call upon your personal experiences to help you flesh out their message. Besides your personal experience, you should incorporate universal archetypes and symbolism to deliver a reading that accurately captures the cards' messages.

The Experimental Approach

Cartomancy is a field that has continued to evolve over time. This implies that new methods and technologies are being crafted daily to take advantage of reading the cards' information. When you're working with the experimental approach, it means that you must keep an open and receptive mind, one that is willing to think outside of the box. It means that you must be willing to adapt to the times. These days, everything is digital. Therefore, you must be willing to accept that digital readings can be and indeed are valid.

The experimental approach to reading cards means you must work with technology to see how it can help you. This means creating digital tools and platforms your end user can easily access to get the necessary information they seek. The upside to working with technology is that you do not necessarily need to be present for your querent to get a reading. If the end user of your digital platform is in touch with their intuition and keeps an open mind, there is nothing to worry about. Their reading will be as accurate and useful as that from an in-person, traditional cartomancy session. Naturally, the energies of the spiritual world, which permeate everything, will also work through the programming and deliver the messaging required by the querent.

Being an experimentalist also implies that you should be at peace with creating new spreads to tackle unique situations. Sure, you have been offered a plethora of ways that you can work with cards. However, that does not mean you cannot create your own spreads. After all, the common spreads used today were created by someone, weren't they? So, as an experimental cartomancer, nothing stops you from doing your own thing if you find it more efficient. You must ensure that you're working with your intuition to create the right spread or make the right changes at the right time contextually. For instance, you may be intuitively led to combine several systems uniquely, giving you much deeper insight into far more comprehensive readings than usual.

Experimentalist cartomancy also implies working collaboratively. You may have to work with other readers and practitioners to interpret the cards. This could be beneficial because other readers may have certain pieces of the puzzle that you may have been missing from your own interpretations, or it may help you see things in a new light that you find beneficial to your own readings going forward.

Another interesting thing with the experimental approach to cartomancy is that you can work with artistic elements to help you better divine your card's messages. This could include designing new forms of cards that add interesting elements to a reading. You may even want to incorporate visuals and performative art, which is possible thanks to new technologies.

Being able to personalize your practice is a key tenet of experimental cartomancy. In other words, you should create certain routines, rituals, and methodologies that work for you in particular rather than go along with a general prescription for this craft. When you personalize practice like this, it enhances your results. You'll find that your readings are very accurate, and you seldom have to wonder what the cards say because you have a proven, working system.

Finally, there's the unmistakable aspect of constant research and exploration. This means combing through the old ways of doing things and looking at emerging technologies and methodologies to craft newer, better ways of receiving information from the spirit realm through the cards.

Figuring Out Your Approach

Suppose you're wondering what the best approach to take is regarding cartomancy. In that case, it will depend on your beliefs about the craft and your goals and preferences. For one thing, you must self-reflect. Think about the things that interest you and where your strengths lie. Think about whether you're more of an analytical thinker (which means the analytical approach is for you) or if you do better with your feeling (which could imply that you should be better as an intuitive cartomancer). Suppose you are inclined toward therapeutic work and love to tinker and experiment. That should tell you that you would do well with a blend of therapeutic and experimental approaches.

The next thing you must do is to get familiar with the various approaches. This means you will have to read several books, watch videos on YouTube, and do intense research to figure out the different philosophies surrounding cartomancy because there are many. You can even attend workshops and take courses to learn from experienced people to see what floats your boat. This exploration period will help you determine the different perspectives and develop your unique blend of approaches.

It is important to note that there will be an inevitable trial-and-error phase where you try to see what works and what doesn't. It will help if you continue practicing and noting what works for you. Notice how your experience goes and how connected you feel to the cards and the reading process. Pay attention to how much more accurate you are when using one methodology over another. You'll inevitably craft your unique method of working with the cards by constantly experimenting like this.

It would be remiss not to mention that your intuition will be a big factor here. So, you should always trust the guidance you get from within as you work to determine your approach. If you feel something is wrong for you, don't hesitate to drop it. If it works, it should be a part of your cartomancy arsenal.

Having someone to act as your mentor would be helpful. Work with those who are more experienced than you are. Seek out communities of those doing the same thing as you are, and you will find yourself getting better at what you do and gradually creating a niche for yourself. Now, what are you going to do with all this information? The ball is in your court. May Spirit guide you on your journey with the cards!

Conclusion

You've finally come to the end of this book, and at this point, you should know enough about cartomancy for you to begin your journey. Remember that this is something that requires your intuition to take the lead. This means you must approach the practice with trust and faith. Have a lot of curiosity and zero expectations about how it will play out for you.

Many beginners fall into the trap of feeling frustrated and angry with themselves because they are not getting the results that they had hoped for. You mustn't fall into this trap. This craft, like any other skill, will take time to learn. Therefore, be patient with yourself, and trust that the more you work with your intuition, just like any muscle, the stronger it will get.

Cartomancy is a powerful skill that you can use to better not just your life but the lives of those around you. It is a worthy endeavor to be a part of, and the fact that you have chosen this book and read it through to this point indicates that you must be called to practice this craft. Whenever you feel frustrated about your results, remember that it's not a matter of *if* you'll get better – but *when*.

There is no point in reading this book if you do not practice what you've learned! Just because you understand how something works does not mean you are automatically a professional. In the same way, you would not expect to be a professional driver just by reading a book about driving or watching a video. You have to put in the work yourself.

Therefore, you should get your first deck and get to know your cards as soon as possible. When things finally start to click, you'll wonder how you could ever have lived without consulting the cards!

Here's another book by Mari Silva that you might like

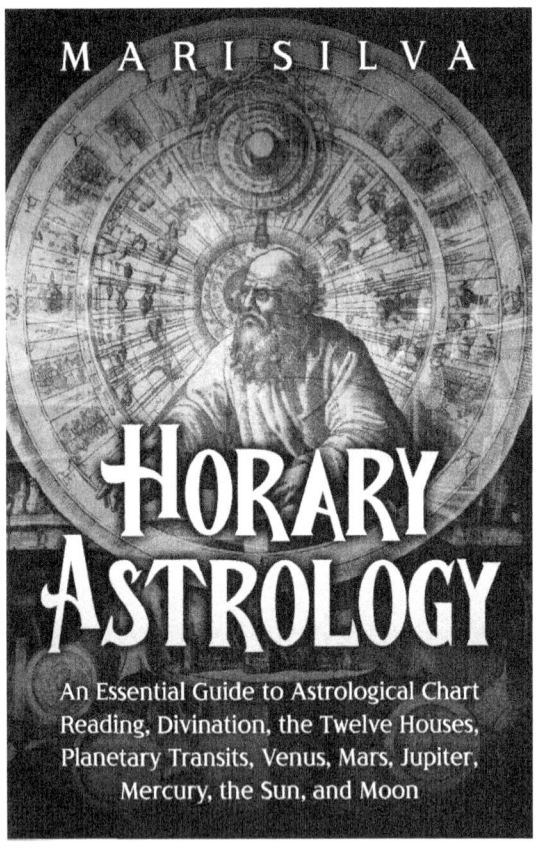

Your Free Gift
(only available for a limited time)

Thanks for getting this book! If you want to learn more about various spirituality topics, then join Mari Silva's community and get a free guided meditation MP3 for awakening your third eye. This guided meditation mp3 is designed to open and strengthen ones third eye so you can experience a higher state of consciousness. Simply visit the link below the image to get started.

https://spiritualityspot.com/meditation

Or, Scan the QR code!

References

Caldwell, R. (2019). Brief history of cartomancy. Academia.edu.
https://www.academia.edu/6477311/Brief_history_of_cartomancy

Cicero, C., & Cicero, S. T. (2011). The Essential Golden Dawn: An Introduction to High Magic. Llewellyn Publications.

Decker, R., Depaulis, T., & Dummett, M. (1996). A Wicked Pack of Cards: The Origins of the Occult Tarot. St. Martin's Press.

Decker, R., & Dummett, M. (2013). The History of the Occult Tarot. Prelude Books.

Dunn, P. (2013). Cartomancy with the Lenormand and the Tarot: Create Meaning and Gain Insight from the Cards. Llewellyn Worldwide.

DuQuette, L.M. (2003). Understanding Aleister Crowley's Thoth Tarot. Weiser Books.

Greer, M. K. (2002). Tarot for Your Self: A Workbook for Personal Transformation. New Page Books.

Huson, P. (2004). Mystical Origins of the Tarot: From Ancient Roots to Modern Usage. Destiny Books.

Katz, M., & Goodwin, T. (2011). Around the Tarot in 78 Days: A Personal Journey Through the Cards. Llewellyn Publications.

Keen. (n.d.). Playing card meanings in cartomancy. Keen Articles. Retrieved from https://www.keen.com/articles/tarot/cartomancy-card-meanings

Kliegman, S. (2011). Cartomancy with the Lenormand and the Tarot: Create Meaning & Gain Insight from the Cards. Llewellyn Publications.

Matthews, C. (2014). The Complete Lenormand Oracle Handbook: Reading the Language and Symbols of the Cards. Destiny Books.

McNutt, A., Crisan, A., & Correll, M. (2020, April). Divining insights: Visual analytics through cartomancy. In Extended Abstracts of the 2020 CHI Conference on Human Factors in Computing Systems.

Moore, J. (2012). Cartomancy – Fortune Telling With Playing Cards (Speed Learning Book 1). Kindle Edition.

Moore, B. (2012). Tarot Spreads: Layouts & Techniques to Empower Your Readings. Llewellyn Worldwide.

Nichols, S. (1980). Jung and Tarot: An archetypal journey. Weiser Books.

Pollack, R. (1997). Seventy-Eight Degrees of Wisdom: A Book of Tarot. Thorsons.

Stackpole, M. A. (2006). Cartomancy: Book Two of The Age of Discovery. Spectra.

Waite, A.E. (1910). The Pictorial Key to the Tarot. Rider & Company

Printed in Great Britain
by Amazon